'Hodkinson has an evocative turn economy of language and the writing flows effortlessly.'
Luke Bainbridge, *The Observer*

'He writes quite beautifully, which means that those of us with lesser gifts are given a glimpse into his soul. It is a richly rewarding place to be.' Richard Whitehead, *The Times*

'You can almost see the mist on the moors above the ground and the rain lashing the chimneys of disused mills. Rochdale was not a pretty place then, nor is it now.'
Michael Henderson, *The Guardian*

'It all sounds like a grim *Monty Python* parody of a Northern upbringing. But it doesn't read that way. Hodkinson has a light touch and a modest, self-effacing style which he deploys to discover humour in the unlikeliest of places.'
Andrew Baker, *Daily Telegraph*

'Hodkinson has crafted an emotive tale of youthful hope that's so utterly believable.' Ben Myers, *Mojo*

'*The Last Mad Surge of Youth* is a novel set in the music business that's both free of cliché and acutely on the money: Rock Novel of the Year.' Mark Blake, *Q*

'He writes with economy and elegance, self-deprecating but never self-pitying.' Tom Dart, *The Times*

'A deft writer, poignant and funny at different times.'
Harry Pearson, *The Guardian*

www.markhodkinson.com

By the same author:

LIFE AT THE TOP
(Queen Anne Press, 1998)

BLUE MOON
(Mainstream Publishing, 1999)

LIFE SENTENCE
(Parrs Wood Press, 2001)

BELIEVE IN THE SIGN
(Pomona, 2007)

THE LAST MAD SURGE OF YOUTH
(Pomona, 2009)

SPOTLAND: THE SUN ALSO RISES

Spotland: The Sun Also Rises
(and other football stories)

MARK HODKINSON

POMONA

A Pomona Book

P-021

Published by Pomona Books 2010
Telephone 01422 846900 · e-mail admin@pomonauk.co.uk

www.pomonauk.co.uk

I

A CIP catalogue record for this book
is available from the British Library

978-1-904590-28-6

Cover design by Geoff Read

Set in Monotype Bembo Book
Typeset by Christian Brett

Printed and bound in England by
CPI Cox & Wyman, Reading, RG1 8EX

For George and Alec

Acknowledgements

The author wishes to thank: Richard Whitehead, Christian Brett, Geoff Read, Tom Harrison, Daniel Youngs, Stu Ashworth, Andy Hollis, Paula Ridings, Boff Whalley, Luke Bainbridge, David Pugh, Trevor Hoyle, John McDonough, James Heward, James Wallace, David Chappell, Keith Blackmore, Matt Dickinson, Michael Hann, Chris Dunphy, Col Cavanagh, David Taylor, Fred Eyre, Eugenio Gonzalez, Graham Morris, Guy Patrick, Jim Stringer, Victor Collinge, George and Ben Kelsall, John Wallace, Jonathan Dillon, Kester Aspden, Tom Palmer, Mark Wilbraham, Miles Moss, Kevin Sampson, Tim Hallissey, Richard Lysons, John Abraham, Dave Roberts, Alessandro Gallenzi and, of course, my dad, without whom …

The features from *The Times* are reproduced with the kind permission of News International Ltd.

PART ONE

Spotland: The Sun Also Rises

I

PART TWO

And Other Football Stories

75

1. Interviews

77

2. Broken Idols

111

3. Close to the Edge

139

4. The Beautiful Game?

165

5. The Business of Football

189

Preface

Until this season just gone (2009/10) I thought I'd written all that was possible about Rochdale AFC and the lives interwoven within and around it. I had published two books about the club (*Life Sentence* and *Believe in the Sign*) and I was going to move on, write about other things. Then it happened. Our eternal story of losing and struggling and fighting for survival changed. We started winning. We continued winning. We secured promotion. And Rochdale being promoted is not the same as it happening to any other club. On average, most experience promotion or relegation every five years or so but we have been stuck in the basement division of the Football League for 36 years. To help put this in perspective, Darlington, until their relegation this season, were the second longest serving members of the division with 18 years, the lightweights. My dad, a fellow devotee, has a favourite saying, the one about every dog having its day. But this was more than a day; it was a whole season. To exaggerate only slightly, this was sunshine at midnight, the Rochdale Canal flowing with molten gold.

So, people asked: are you going to write about the promotion? At last I had an opportunity to write about joy, and hope fulfilled. Typically, a calamitous end-of-season run shaded grey the edges of this riot of colour but, whatever, we were up, up and away. Most of all, I wanted to put down a marker, an 'I was here'. I collect and love Rochdale AFC memorabilia. I like that it forms a portal to the past. I want someone 10, 20, 30 years from now to pick up this book and view it as a literary time capsule: this is how it was when Rochdale won promotion, for this particular bloke, his dad and his kids.

I make no claim to be Rochdale's keenest supporter. I go to all the home games and the away ones within 100 miles or so. This rough geographical limit means, for example, that I wasn't one of the 213 Dale fans at Aldershot on a very cold Tuesday night in January, 2010. To them, respect. I attend home games with my son, George, aged 13, and my dad, who now qualifies for a concessionary season ticket. My other son, Alec, aged 11, is selective about his trips to Spotland or away games, which I respect him for: clearly a bright lad.

This isn't one of those down-the-line souvenir books, a collection of facts and figures and lovely photos. I'm sure these will follow and I'll definitely be buying them. It's a personal perspective, one that has been shaped by watching Rochdale every one of those 36 seasons in Division Four (or what ever they choose to call it). This means I've seen the truly bad times — two seasons at the bottom of the Football League; 26 occasions when the attendance at Spotland was below 1,000; crisis meetings in pubs and clubs where collection buckets were passed round. You don't forget that as a kid, your club under threat of closure. I'm aware that I sometimes seem jaundiced, especially when I talk to George who, in his few years of supporting the club, has known relative success. He wants me to let the past go. So do I.

We — Rochdale fans introduced to the club since 1974 — have no experience of the sense of well being that success engenders. Ours has been support without real justification. Sure, we have won matches, had cup runs and played well occasionally but there has been no moving on, moving up. We have stayed put and believed it was our destiny to remain marooned between mediocrity and failure, playing the same teams on the same grounds again and again.

The 2009/10 season taught us differently. All those years now feel to be a linear journey rather than a circular one. It has become, in the space of 10 months, August to May, a paean to belief, loyalty and hope. I am happy at Spotland, among the people there, because we share these values and we each know they have been hard to maintain down the years. We've been mocked, made to feel foolish. Our team has hurt us, embarrassed us. It has made us too dark perhaps, too knowing, but this season has shown us that success can come to all; it is as much part of life as disappointment. Finally, the sun also rises.

The pieces that form 'And Other Football Stories' are drawn mainly from *The Times* newspaper. For several years the paper had the motif, 'Under the skin of sport'. Slogans such as these are often cheap currency, empty words, but here they were a truth. The brief was to find the offbeat, the colour, the characters. I was trusted to 'write it as you find it' and given nothing but wholehearted support. The features are reprinted here as they appeared in the paper, with only minor editing. I have taken the opportunity to provide extra insight or updates here and there. It is surprising how many of them have links to Rochdale AFC. I'm not sure what that says about me.

Mark Hodkinson
August, 2010

PART ONE

Spotland: The Sun Also Rises

August, 2009

A summer barely worthy of the name passes us by. At least the rain was a bit warmer than usual. The three-month break from football and Rochdale AFC hadn't reinvigorated me. I was tired, still in last season's clothes. This was my 36th year as a Rochdale fan; I'd learned not to dance across the carpet when the calendar struck August. We had made the League Two Play-off final two years before at Wembley, losing 3–2 to Stockport County. And in 2008/09 we lost to Gillingham in the Play-off semi-final. There you go, then: final to semi-final and all set to start a new season with practically the same squad of players — clear, indisputable evidence that we were slipping back to staying put.

Most of us had believed that appearing at Wembley would be the apogee of our support; it was downhill from here. One Dale fanatic who had followed them passionately for 40 years was so convinced of this that he made it the catalyst to end his support. He broke the tie and moved on. I was envious of his resolve. I wanted to be him, living a life divorced from the fortunes of this cruel club. I became lost to reverie: for how long would you still check the scores? What did you do when the team was playing — how did you displace your thoughts, the longing to be at the ground? When did you forget to remember that they were actually playing on a certain day? What did you do with your life? I was told he had moved to a rural area far from Spotland. I saw him walking down dirt tracks, among dry stone walls, throwing rocks into streams. This solitary figure, lost.

How heavy was his heart? And while I was imagining all this, I then thought how daft it was to feel this way, about a daft team playing a daft opening match of the season at Port Vale. What did it matter? Nothing and everything: that was the problem.

Football fans place far too much emphasis on the first game of the season. In it they are convinced they see the rest of their season distilled. I didn't go to Port Vale because I was still sulking about losing out to Gillingham in the play-offs. And I'd been to Port Vale the previous season when we had lost 2–1 three days after Christmas, conceding a late goal. Unhappy Christmas. I didn't like returning so soon to places where I had been made to feel miserable, annoyed. The journey home afterwards was too fresh in my mind, that irritable feeling in the stomach. There was no point in going there again and jabbing at an old wound.

I listened to updates from the match on the radio. We took the lead through Joe Thompson. I always like it when Joe scores because it confounds supporters. You can tell within seconds of seeing Joe on a football pitch that he is a *nice* lad. He's even-tempered, plays the game fairly. Many fans want him to get stuck in more, growl at the full back. But Joe has this easy, almost lackadaisical manner about him. He plays as if he's having a kick-about with his young nephews on the park. Such is his demeanour, it can pass you by that he's actually working hard, covering runs, playing simple but effective passes. Some of the Main Stand moaners around me have an almost pathological hatred and holler for him to be taken off almost as soon as he's sighted in his kit. (If they got to the ground early enough, they'd probably shoo him away as he walked across the car park.) The pro-Joes tell them to shut it, give the lad a chance. The anti-Joes tell them no they should shut it; he's had his bloody chance. But when Joe scores we all stand up, cheer and love him as we would a perfect son.

Port Vale equalised and, therefore, we saw our season in miniature. One game, one goal, one conceded, one point. We had a team of triers, probably too good collectively for a relegation scrap but most likely able to summon mid-table mediocrity: that word again. I was glad I'd not gone to Vale Park. There is great satisfaction in knowing you haven't missed anything significant at a football match, such as a win; you made the right decision.

Before I set off for an away game I have to form a rationale of why I should go, aside from the match itself. Basically I have to think of another reason to be there, or several reasons — I don't want to rely on the football alone because it has let me down so many times. This might mean a stop-off at a nearby cathedral or museum, or a trip to the local Frankie & Bennie's. If this isn't possible, I'll focus on how good it is to be travelling with my young son (or sons), able to talk about things in a more languid way than we can through the week when school and Xboxes and their pals interrupt constantly. You can end up at some pretty interesting conversations via a lament on Chris Dagnall missing an open goal or a slow ponder on Nathan Stanton's phobia of crossing the half-way line.

We had two good supplementary reasons to watch Rochdale play Sheffield Wednesday at Hillsborough in the first round of the League Cup. Firstly I wanted George to visit a large ground steeped in history. His life as a football supporter has been spent chiefly at lower league grounds or watching matches on television. The other reason to visit Sheffield was to call on one of my reporter pals, Benny Hill — a decision I was later glad I'd made. I had first met Benny during the 1998/99 season when *The Times* made me a quasi writer-in-residence at Oakwell,

Barnsley, from where I had to contribute a weekly column to the paper.

Benny, now retired, was archetypal old school and far funnier than the comedian of the same name. When we called at his bungalow, although poorly, he showed George through to his 'study' where he kept scrapbooks and files, and talked to him about Barnsley players from years gone by. Afterwards we had tea and cake with Benny and his wife, Dinah, and I was glad George had come across this piece of history, too: a down-to-earth, time-served journalist steeped in football knowledge but still as enthusiastic as a kid. As we left and headed to Hillsborough, Benny said:

"They're not up to much, tha knows, Wednesday. Tha may get a result there, tonight."

We didn't get a result. We lost 3–0, a scoreline that flattered us. Matches against teams from higher divisions are played in the mind as much as the feet. Players have to remain indifferent to the size of the stands around them and the stature of the players before them. Rochdale played with fear. They jabbed the ball backwards and sideways all evening. When play broke into Wednesday's half, we snatched at shots. On the way out of Hillsborough I struck up a conversation with a Dale fan I knew.

"They weren't up to much, were they?" I said.

"I expected it, to be honest."

"Why?"

"Well, Wednesday are a Championship side, aren't they?"

His attitude irritated me. Walking back to the car, I realised, absurd as it may seem, that I had never gone to see Rochdale play and *expected* that they would lose. I always believed that today was our day, no matter who we were playing and what past experience had supposedly taught me. And I always resented the players, and fans, for any courtship with defeatism or acceptance of 'rightful place'. I'm with Eminem on this one when he says at the tail-out of *Lose Yourself*: 'You can do anything if you set your mind to it.' Buy that lad a tray of pie and peas, double gravy.

Four days after losing at Hillsborough, a last-minute penalty by Tom Kennedy against Aldershot at Spotland earned us our first win of the season. The following Tuesday we lost at home to Cheltenham Town 1–0 after dominating the match. Predictably, their goal came in the last minute, scored by a rehabilitated Julian Alsop, one of the division's most celebrated 'lumps of wood' (i.e.: big striker of limited pace and ability but effective as nuisance value). The goal came after Marcus Holness was robbed of the ball close to the half-way line. It was practically his only mistake of the game but led to a defeat. Their manager, Martin Allen, talked afterwards about how his team had dug in, stayed solid, stuck to their game plan. It was manager-speak for bloody lucky; they all did it.

I didn't go to the match away at Rotherham United for the inverse reason to the one that stopped me travelling to Port Vale. Two years before, I had seen Rochdale put in a consummate performance at Millmoor, playing shrewd, enterprising football. We had won 4–2 and our dominance was so complete that I knew that no matter how many times I might travel to Rotherham — or wherever Rotherham United FC happened to be based, such were their nomadic tendencies — it was inconceivable that Rochdale would play so well there again. We had also just sold Adam Le Fondre to Rotherham and the absolute rule of football was that ex-players always scored against their old club. This has happened so often to Rochdale that before some games I have considered what I would prefer:

to lose 1−0 and our ex-player *not* score or draw 1−1 and him to score. I think I'd take the defeat, merely to scupper the hoodoo of the returning ex-hero.

We lost 2−1. Adam Le Fondre scored. I was at a friend's house at the time, embroiled in the cricket: England were on the verge of winning the Ashes. The league table came up on the television screen. We were 18th. Suddenly I felt far, far away from Rochdale AFC. Wembley, losing to Gillingham, this awful start to the new season: that's it; I'm giving up on hope. And when you've given up, nothing can hurt you. You can convince yourself that they're not your team, nothing to do with you (wouldn't you be with the other Daleys at the Don Valley Stadium if it were your team?). But why did it still hurt and why did life, all those little things you think and feel and see through a day, feel less good now they'd lost? How stupid to have your feelings governed by something that happened within a chalked-off rectangle of grass between a group of men who didn't even know you existed. I decided: I've got a season ticket now so I might as well go to the games but I'll work up some indifference, a shrug, a take-it-or-leave-it approach. Otherwise this lot are going to make me bloody ill, if I'm not already.

Bury, next. Local derby. It didn't matter now about the league and the rest of the season. That could wait. This was close-up and personal. On one of the Rochdale websites someone had turned their manager, Alan Knill, into a rat, complete with twitchy nose. We knew of Knill mainly through his interviews on *BBC Radio Manchester* where he often sounded like an executive for a corporate brand, doing that blandspeak where to heed criticism was believed to reveal vulnerability. Our manager, Keith Hill, did this too, but not as effectively: he often tied himself in knots or — as he did on one infamous occasion — embarked instead upon an extended metaphor on pornography. Knill's confidence teetered on arrogance, his brashness on belligerence. Football wasn't supposed to be about personalities and getting one over on anyone but if I were a player or manager I'd want to beat Alan Knill's team, hardcore.

We'd not recorded a win against Bury at Spotland for 16 years. Keith Hill believed we made too much fuss about the fixture. We didn't believe he made *enough* fuss about it. We won 3−0. The final goal, a penalty, was scored by Tom Kennedy, Bury-born, boyhood Bury fan, ex-Bury player, whose dad, Keith Kennedy, had also played for Bury. His celebrations might have been expected to be muted considering such close links to the town and club. To hell with diplomacy. Kennedy ran almost the full length of the away stand, cupping his ears, stretching out his arms. Understandably, the Bury fans went mad. They ran at the fence. One galloped on to the pitch. I smiled at Kennedy's effrontery but as I did I was thinking that his actions could lead to crowd trouble. As a professional footballer he was afforded protection but if a kid walking home from the match was attacked in Edenfield Road, how much of that hostility had been stirred up by our irresponsible full back?

Later that evening Kennedy's 'celebration' was highlighted on the *Football League Show*. The condemnation was fervent. They made no attempt to place his actions in context (apparently some of the abuse Kennedy received from Bury fans before the goal was nasty) and instead indulged in that gleeful sanctimony particular to television, where they pretend something is shameful and offensive but take great pleasure in picking through it, again and again. By the end I started to enjoy rewinding Kennedy's come-on to the shook-up shakers. I told my sons, however, that it was childish and reckless and then asked them to help me load up the footage into my mobile phone.

September, 2009

Keith Hill isn't bothered about cup matches. That's what they say. It was true that our record in cup competitions had been poor under Hill, though it seemed peevish to point this out when you consider how much the club had improved in his stewardship. In the first round of the Johnstone's Paint Trophy against Bradford City he made a bizarre team selection. When David Flitcroft was at his peak he was often referred to euphemistically as 'well-fed' or 'stocky'. Now 35 and with only one first-team game to his name in two seasons, he was even better fed and stockier. Still, Dale's assistant manager was chosen in midfield against Bradford at Spotland, with kit man Jack Northover presumably sent out to find suitably voluminous shorts.

Although well loved, Flitcroft's appearance gave the match a sense of the circus and the more serious-minded among us felt a little cheated as Bradford ran out 2–1 winners and Dale exited another cup competition at an early stage. Keith Hill isn't bothered about cup matches. That's what they say.

Morecambe, on a Friday night. Summer had gone now; the light was different and the air carried a chill. The win against Bury had lifted Rochdale fans out of their homes and down the motorway to the seaside. We sat in the Main Stand at Christie Park, in facilities decades out of date. We were all squashed up. On the pitch we were all spread out, the defenders at sea. By half-time we were 3–0 down. Fans shouted obscenities. One bloke close by was fucking this and fucking that, fucking had enough. I wanted to tell him to shut up but I've seen before what can happen. Suddenly *you're* the focus of his anger instead of the team and you've got to be prepared to fight your corner, stand your ground. It was easier to sit your chin deeper into your scarf, look the other way. Arguing and fighting was unpleasant enough; it was even worse among your own kind. Three minutes into the second half, Chris Dagnall scored. The team was playing with incredible urgency, chasing every ball. Joe Thompson pulled another back and instead of celebrating, he implored his team-mates back to their own half for the re-start. The pressure on Morecambe's goal was relentless. The ball broke to the exquisitely named *Dale* Stevens, on loan from Oldham Athletic, and he fired home. The Dale fans went mental, mad, crazy. Rochdale didn't do comebacks, see. This was new to us — such fighting spirit, sheer willpower. We looked at one another: what's going on here?

The comeback at Morecambe galvanised the team. We won the next four matches: 2−1 against Torquay United at home; 2−1 away at Northampton Town; 4−1 at home against Hereford United and 2−0 at Darlington. Chris Dagnall had scored six goals already. The previous season he'd virtually had to alternate a place in the team with Adam Le Fondre who was a similar type of footballer. The arrangement didn't suit either of them. They both fed off confidence. Their natural game was compromised once they became worried about being picked or under threat of substitution at any minute. Adam was the more accomplished finisher, as his goal tally for Rotherham testified, but Dagnall was the harder worker, able to better 'defend from the front', so beloved of modern managers. Dagnall had also quickly formed a partnership with new loan signing, Chris O'Grady.

We went to the match at Darlington, driving up there in the

late afternoon. The trip was largely justified because Rochdale were on form but, I have to concede, there was a morbid fascination in visiting a £20 million stadium housing considerably less than one-tenth of its capacity. We moan at Rochdale (oh, we moan) but sometimes consider ourselves fortunate. We are thankful not to have gone the same way as Workington Town, Southport, Newport County, Wimbledon, Maidstone United or Halifax Town who, for what ever reason, left the Football League and have not yet returned. I often think of their supporters and imagine that they must look on Rochdale with envy. While we might have been starved of success, we have always been a reasonably well-run club and this was an area outside the reach of most supporters: we simply had to trust.

Approaching the Northern Echo Darlington Arena (its sixth name in six years), it was impossible not to feel sorry for their supporters drawn unwittingly into this folly. How foolish or gullible, or both, must the men trusted with the club have been to allow George Reynolds, a man well-known for his criminal past, to make the club his play-thing? I stared up to the glass palace above the main entrance, at the busybody uniformed staff going about their business as if they were settling down passengers on an ocean liner, knowing full well that it would never set sail.

Rochdale's win took us into second place, behind Bournemouth. The defeat meant Darlington had not recorded a win in the first 10 matches of the season and were already rooted to the bottom of the league, where they would remain.

(Unknown to most Dale fans, the club had suffered its own financial problems through the summer of 2009. The situation had escalated until HM Revenue and Customs had issued a winding up order for unpaid bills in the Companies Court. On September 23 the club released a statement on the official website assuring supporters that the matter was being dealt with and the debts cleared. It was manifest that the sale of Le Fondre had been essential and this was the reason why the club had made no real attempt to fend off Rotherham's interest.)

The four wins and a draw from five games in September led to Keith Hill being chosen as the Coca-Cola League Two manager of the month.

October, 2009

As a kid I didn't care much for the structure of football grounds or consider their aesthetic quality. I went for the atmosphere: the singing, the shouting, the sense of belonging to a crowd. At home matches I positioned myself behind the goal at the Sandy Lane end, pressed up close to the perimeter wall. I wanted to be in that exact position so much that I was often in situ an hour before the kick-off. It meant that I saw very little of the movement of play because I was low down and peering through the netting and goalkeeper's legs. When the ball hit the net, however, I had the best view in the ground. Suddenly, the game became 3D and I had to remind myself not to flinch or move out of the way because the net would stop the ball – and how magnificently! – in its progress. Bodies would tumble down the terraces behind me and I'd hug Glen Beard or Mark Hollinrake or Gary Ashworth or whoever else was with me. I'd imagine, just for those few seconds, that the next stage of this utter joy was levitation.

Now I'm all grown-up I can do without 'atmosphere'. I love the game as much as ever but in a different way. I want to see the detail of a match, the minutiae as well as the goals. And I want to see it from a good angle, preferably looking down from somewhere close to the half-way line. My experience of grounds belonging to clubs that were recently non-League has taught me that this is too much to ask — a decent vantage point and a roof over my head. In reaching the League, clubs such as Macclesfield Town and Accrington Stanley have clearly neglected hospitality in favour of channelling finance into players' wages. One wonders what the League must specify to allow entry: 'Sure, you can leave 1,000 people in the pouring rain on an uncovered terrace but you're not getting a certificate of membership unless the fluorescent ink on Signs A and B is of sufficient lead-density.' So, I boycotted our visit to League new-boys Burton Albion where we lost 1–0 and I didn't find out whether they provided a roof or not. I had an antipathy to these non-League interlopers on principle [see page 157] and to lose against them was hurt upon the hurt of the usual. Once again, I'd got lucky with my match selection.

Another penalty by Tom Kennedy, making his 100th Rochdale appearance, helped earn us a 2–1 home win against Barnet. After the game Keith Hill became aware of criticism from some supporters (no one was sure who exactly) and revealed his tetchy side:

"Some of the football was garbage when I was a player here [he made 176 appearances for Rochdale between 1996 and 2001] and it got the reaction from the terraces it deserved. What I find very difficult to understand is why some supporters still find it in themselves to moan now. We are playing a brand of football I'd like to watch as a supporter, a brand that is high tempo and positive and I'd like to think the mood from the stands would match this ethos."

This had been a running issue through Hill's managerial reign — a tendency to over-react to criticism usually made by a handful of fans who would, if Dale signed them, find fault in Messi ('He can't bloody tackle') and Rooney ('Useless overweight sod').

Our next match was away at Grimsby Town, a team, much the same as Darlington, who had started the season in woeful form, winning once in their first 11 matches. We travelled up there early and parked on the seafront at Cleethorpes. A great expanse of grey mud separated us from the water. George and me jogged across it until our feet began sinking and we doubled back. It felt bizarre: on a beach and then, an hour or so later, at a football match. How different the world can seem when you come at something from a different direction. I thought of our regular redbrick route to Spotland, through Deeplish, past Asda, down Mellor Street and the abandoned mills and work-shops; this little journey I have made every two weeks for most of my life.

We beat Grimsby 2−0 with goals from Adam Rundle and Chris O'Grady. Rochdale fans, who each carry with them a rucksack full of inferiority issues, find it difficult to be imperi-ous. We know too well the converse of this, what it is to have people look down upon us. All the same, the win against Grimsby, a hitherto bigger and more successful club than us, felt *routine*. You sensed we were always in the ascendancy and that Grimsby would toil without reward because an invisible force (confidence? self-belief?) was at work within our team, our club, and each of us sitting in that ramshackle stand behind the goal, a mile or so from the muddy beach.

It is impossible not to admire Accrington Stanley's manager, John Coleman. If someone compiled a graph factoring in budget and average home attendance to achievement, he would probably be the most successful manager, pro-rata, in England. He is a tough little bugger who tells it straight. Last season, after Rochdale had beaten his team, he told the local press that it wasn't a disastrous result because Rochdale fancied themselves as a promotion side. The key word here is *fancied*. He was imply-ing that Rochdale had ideas above their station; he knew full well the irritation this would cause. Clearly, he had watched Rochdale vigilantly, even to the extent of making them play towards the Sandy Lane end in the first-half, knowing this would affect their usual rhythm of play. Stanley played aggressively and nudged Rochdale from their favoured passing game, running out 2−1 winners — their first win at Spotland since 1956.

Keith Hill provoked the Bournemouth fans before Rochdale's visit there by, once more, criticising clubs who had entered administration. He had identified that some clubs were interpreting League rules on a strategic basis. They were prepared to overspend — thereby loading their squads with better players than their competitors — in the hope that promotion or the avoidance of relegation would allow them to settle their debts retrospectively. If their strategy floundered they clearly took the view that the mandatory points deduction (twice in Bournemouth's case, being docked 10 points in February 2008 and 17 before the 2008/09 season) was a punishment they could stand. In other words, it not only made the risk worthwhile, it tacitly encouraged it.

When Bournemouth entered administration in February 2008 they were reportedly £4 million in debt. Afterwards, reformed under new ownership (with the same name, at the same ground with the same players and the same fans in the same club colours and with the same League status), they were ordered to pay back 10p for every pound they owed. This effectively meant that in the trading period preceding administration they were purchasing everything at a 90 per cent discount. The full list of creditors is probably filed somewhere and, no doubt, will include formal institutions such as the Inland Revenue, HM Customs and Revenue, and various financial institutions, alongside the disparate rag-tag of supporting services to a football club: programme printers, pie suppliers, laundry, kit manufacturers etc. Now, football clubs always try to ensure the players' wages are met because if they are not, they will leave, the team is weakened, and they fall down the League. While Bournemouth and others were not paying the various bodies and individuals, they were able to divert funds to wages in greater sums (thereby attracting the better players) while Rochdale et al, by virtue of paying their bills, had a limit placed on how much they had available for transfer fees and wages.

Understandably, the local papers in Bournemouth were agitated by Hill's comments. Neil Meldrum, writing in the *Bournemouth Evening Echo*, said (in a suitably themed piece): 'Hill has stoked the fires to such an extent, he must have been Guy Fawkes in a previous life.' Bournemouth's defender Warren Cummings took a break from polishing the halo that encircles his club to remark:

'It does surprise me that, in the lead up to a game, any manager would talk about things that are out of their control at another club. One thing is for sure, though, players and management at this club would never comment negatively about any other football club and I think that's the right way to be. If people want to do it about us, we can only use it to our advantage.'

In the event, they didn't. Rochdale beat the league-leaders 4–0, playing some wonderfully compelling football. It was a categorical indication that Rochdale were having a very un-Rochdale season.

After the game it was alleged that Hill had made 'gestures' to the home fans or the directors or maybe a passing seagull. No one was quite sure whether he'd blown a raspberry to the Mayor of Bournemouth or merely shook his right hand very fast as if freeing salt from a salted up saltcellar. Either way, the rumour of what he may or may not have done to mark his team's wonderful victory was another excuse for the local media to forge the eccentric Mr Hill as Beelzebub's best mate.

November, 2009

Each year, on the first or second Saturday in November, we become an everyday (football-free) family. The tradition began a few years ago when we decided to mark George's birthday by going to the seaside for the weekend. It would be too much to eschew a home match, of course, so we pick which ever weekend that sees Rochdale play away. We wrap up well and walk along the beach, peering into rock pools and, out to sea, at the passing ocean liners. Then we climb the steep cobbled lane from the sea and eat at a café overhanging a brook. All the while, I'm doing what all football folk pretending to be non-football folk do: I'm wondering how my team is doing. I'm cursing that shop after shop is selling fishing nets and fancy shells. A small harbour town like this should be able to boast at least one single bloody television store where I (and others like me) can head to at 4.50pm to see how our team has done. Today, we're playing away at Luton Town in the first round of the FA Cup.

Over the years the FA Cup has often been something to dread for Rochdale fans. Between 1972 and 1983 we were knocked out in the first round seven times by non-League clubs. During this run Grantham beat us 5−3 at Spotland and Telford United, 4−1. On a more positive note, we made the fifth round in 1989/90 and 2002/03, losing to Crystal Palace and Wolverhampton Wanderers respectively. Last season we were beaten 2−0 by Forest Green Rovers after Hill appeared to field a weakened team.

I did not find out the score at Kenilworth Road until half-time. We were on our way back home and had parked in a country lane while we had something to eat. After the Bournemouth victory I knew not to expect the same again. Luton would be all-out to humble a League club, so a 0-0 at half-time would do, followed by a late winning goal for Dale, all neat and tidy. The score came on the radio: Luton Town 3, Rochdale 0. Must be some mistake. I rang dad:

"Are they playing the youth team again mixed with a few of the cleaning ladies?"

No, he informed me, it was the usual team. I stared out forlornly. A mist was tumbling over the fields, the afternoon forward-rolling into evening. Crows bickered in trees above me. Three-nil down to a bloody non-League team. I could already sense the humiliation: the fuss on the radio and television afterwards. It wouldn't matter that Luton had only just dropped out of the League and were, by most measurements, a bigger club than ourselves. We were holding the torch for the Football League, the chosen ones, the giants, and we were about to be toppled by these assumed-to-be minnows. We got a goal back, then another. Come on, the Dale. Just one more, *one more*. The reception on the radio was intermittent. Crackle, shrill, snatch of distant voice. This continued for another 30 miles until the final scores began coming through. Results were read out but still no word on Rochdale. Finally, almost as an afterthought: Luton Town 3, Rochdale 3. I banged the steering wheel, shouted out loud. Joe Thompson had scored with virtually the last kick of the game. Good old Joe. Up the Dale. I knew never to forsake them, to always believe. Here we go, the comeback kings marching on to Wem-ber-lee.

The replay was hastily arranged for three days' later because ITV4 decided to cover the match live. No doubt influenced by the late comeback and the relative goal feast, they expected the same again (clearly showing no understanding of the contrary nature of football). I decided to watch the game on television rather than at Spotland. A few pals have ribbed me about my perceived lack of loyalty on this issue. They feel a 'proper' fan should go to every game, no matter if it is televised or not. I can understand this argument from fans of Premier League clubs but it is different for supporters of lower league sides. Rochdale matches are shown live on television about once every two years. It is a treat to see us treated respectfully on screen; it validates the club and our support. Spotland is a place of mystery to most of us. We only see the stands, the pitch and the players on it. The television cameras take us behind the scenes, into the dressing room and into the tunnel as the players wait to come out. We see the nervous twitches, the stretching and the dancing on the spot, close-ups of their eyes. Afterwards we hear them speak. We realise that Gary Jones is actually Liverpudlian (he's been at the club so long you think of him as a Rochdalian) and that big Chris O'Grady is softly spoken, with kind brown eyes and a polite manner that would delight your mam.

A back injury to Kenny Arthur meant that 16-year-old youth goalkeeper Danny Taberner had to play against Luton Town. He was Rochdale's youngest ever keeper. We dominated the match, creating numerous chances, but lost 2–0. It was the third time in the last four seasons that we'd gone out of the FA Cup in the first round. I was glad I'd stayed at home, in the warm.

We knew the script. Chesterfield were calling at Spotland with former Dale hero, David Perkins, in their team. Perkins had left Dale to sign for Colchester United but had been loaned out after being unable to settle in the south. Many Daleys pined for his return to Spotland in a Dale shirt. While we had grafters in midfield, we didn't have anyone like him who could combine 'ratting' with dribbling skills and a direct style that unsettled opponents.

Chesterfield scored twice but we pulled it back with goals from Chris O'Grady and Craig Dawson. The ball broke in our penalty area to the feet of Perkins. Before he could be closed down, he'd rammed it home. He turned and walked back to his own half without celebrating. He was clapped by the Dale faithful for behaving with such dignity. Dale had lost again but showed plenty of spirit. Fans were also lifted by the debut of goalkeeper, Tom Heaton, who had signed on loan from Manchester United. He had the air of a young man who had been reassured of his talent many times and had come to believe in it wholeheartedly. The confidence he inspired in the defenders was palpable; they each looked at ease knowing they had someone of such ability behind them. Unknown to Dale fans at the time, the defeat to Chesterfield would be the only time they would lose in the 12 games that Heaton was at Spotland.

Before the trip to Dagenham and Redbridge, Rochdale's most celebrated couple, Keith Hill and David Flitcroft, often abbreviated to 'Hillcroft', were asked to switch on the town's Christmas lights. Hillcroft had to share the button-pressing job with (wait for this ...) *X Factor*'s Jamie 'Afro' Archer and Ditchy and Salty from the *Real Radio* Breakfast Show. Hill turned up in a flat cap and scarf but there was no sign of a whippet.

Dagenham and Redbridge were at the top of the table with an unbeaten home record. Rochdale started disastrously, conceding after three minutes. A dogged defensive display kept out the home side and goals from Craig Dawson and Kallum Higginbotham, just a couple of minutes apart in the second half, saw Dale secure a win that few people had expected. The scoreline was repeated three days later when Dale beat moneybags Notts County 2−1 at Spotland with goals from Chris Dagnall (penalty) and Chris O'Grady.

December, 2009

When blokes of a certain age are thrown a football, whether in the garden, on a beach or at the park, they always imagine how easy it would have been to 'make it'— to have been a footballer. If only they'd tried harder, not got involved with girls in their teenage years or not banged their knee at work that time. I mean, it's such a simple game, so easily mastered. Trap it, move it on to your in-step. In their imagination, they're then ghosting past opponents, heading towards goal. Beats one, beats two. Out comes the 'keeper: chipped! And the ball nestles neatly in the net. We're all Matthews or Best or Keegan or Lineker or Beckham or Messi— depending on your age— in our dreams. Of course, it's not like this really. It's a bloody violent sport. You get whacked through every game. You have to run until you feel sick. You have the crowd on your back, another player coveting your position. Only once in a lifetime, perhaps, is football as it can appear in a dream: easy, gentle, effortless, painless, beautiful. We witnessed this very game, all us Daleys, when we saw our team at Valley Parade on December 1, 2010. Some of us even spied the moon turn blue, miles and miles above us in that icy, rainy sky.

We beat Bradford City 3—0, though it could have been eight —even their fans said so. In fact, their good-hearted supporters praised Rochdale as we'd never been praised before. Stuart McCall, their manager, led the communal singing:

"They are far and away the best side we have played all season. We couldn't cope with them. I thought they were outstanding."

Others said we 'out-classed' them. And we did. Their team was left to watch mesmerised as the ball pinged between Rochdale players, across the pitch, down the wings, through the middle. Chris Dagnall scored two, Chris O'Grady one and we missed half a dozen good chances. It was the most complete performance away from home I have ever seen from a Rochdale side and it was also the night a young man guided me to epiphany. As Chris O'Grady turned to celebrate the third goal in the 58th minute, I warned George:

"It's not over yet. Don't celebrate too much."

Quite rightly, he asked what I meant.

"We've thrown away three goal leads before."

He smiled, then asked:

"When?"

"Oh, I can't remember now. I think it was against Port Vale, round about 1981."

"That was ages ago," he said. "How many times have we played since then and it's not happened?"

In an instant I saw both his supreme logic and the absurdity of my pessimism. Sitting in the stand and clawing at a pie seemingly made of tortoise shell, I pondered other things, these hoodoo voodoo things I hold in my head, bad memories I can't shift that do me no good and are of no relevance to anything. And while we're at it, all this nonsense about Football Gods and superstition; I had to shake free of that too, throw the lot in the sea or the River Roach at least. Come on, it's our lads against your lads down there and nothing — *nothing* — else is of any bearing whatsoever, especially Port bloody Vale in 1981. I left Valley Parade a changed man, an improved man, a happier man. Rochdale were top of the league and I had appropriated wisdom from a boy just turned 13 years old.

After the game Chairman Dunphy made a rallying call to the people of Rochdale:

"This team is without doubt the best I have seen in almost 50 years supporting the club and we have a real chance of emulating the promotion of 1969. The football is exciting and a complete joy to watch. My message to anyone stopping at home is to come to Spotland and BE PART OF IT!" You tell 'em, Chris.

Victories against Macclesfield Town (home, 3−0) and Lincoln City (away, 3−1) had a routine feel to them. Up until October 2006 Lincoln away had been a staple of my Dale-supporting season but what happened that day persuaded me never to visit Sincil Bank, or indeed anywhere within a 50-mile range of Lincoln, ever again. It was a warm early-autumn Saturday and we had visited the cathedral, walked around the shops. The sun shone down bright on us until kick-off when the day suddenly turned black, turned horrible. We were trounced 7−1 and every Lincoln attack seemed to finish with a goal. On the walk back to the car after the game I received a text from a close friend: 'Bring back a 7Up for me, will you?' I couldn't raise a snigger. So, this year, I missed the 3−1 win there. No worries, there'll be another victory along very soon.

Fans shifted the snow from the pitch for the home game against Shrewsbury Town. The inevitable Rochdale logic (fatalism by any other name) dictates that when a hardy group of fans embark on a back-breaking night of snow-shovelling the game goes ahead but we lose, so everyone feels not only disappointed but daft too: that game, that defeat, wouldn't have existed if I'd have stayed at home and done something more worthwhile like fiddling about on the pc or flicking through the channels on Sky. The expected didn't happen. Rochdale won 4−0 with two goals each from Craig Dawson and Chris O'Grady. It made for a Happy Christmas: Dale were top of the division, seven points clear. Before this season the only other time I had known Rochdale to be league leaders was a week or two into a new season, when the tables meant very little. If you were top of the division, any division, at Christmas it was a reasonably substantial feat: you meant business.

I hadn't been to Crewe Alexandra for years. They were one of the clubs based relatively close to us we used to play regularly in the 1970s, along with Stockport County and Tranmere Rovers, who had since moved up and left us behind. They each felt to be different clubs now, no longer scruffy strugglers but of the modern age. I had envied them over the years — their promotions, cup runs, the fees they commanded for their players.

I drove with George to the Boxing Day game and arrived an hour before kick-off. I always make sure I'm at grounds early, which is probably a reaction to my dad getting us to places late when I was a kid. He believed maps were for cissies and held no truck with the irrefutable logic of time. It might be 1.45pm and the books say it takes two hours to get from Rochdale to Mansfield but 'Come on, we'll just make it' was his mantra. It wouldn't have mattered so much if he were a mild-mannered man, able to resign himself to possibly missing most of the first-half. No, he was at the windscreen, cursing and shouting, crashing the car into gear, slamming on the brakes. It would take me until half-time to calm down and start to enjoy the game.

On the walk around the ground at Crewe we came across a shack where football programmes were being sold. I went inside and was transported back to 1974 when I'd begun my own collection. The place smelled musty and damp and lovely. Three or four earnest chaps in sensible jackets were behind the counter talking about the toilet facilities at Northampton Town and the ticketing arrangements for the away game at Shrewsbury — proper football blokes. This was my boyhood world come back to life: rusty staples, polythene bags, the word 'bundles' written in felt tip on a ripped up piece of cardboard. I spied a 'sale' section where what looked to be about 15 programmes were inserted into one of those bags with clear plastic on one side and crinkly white paper on the other, the type sometimes used to wrap sweets. And, boy, were they wrapping up something sweet: a decent girth of match programmes from various clubs each worth about £2.50 individually but going for a sale price, the lot of them, for £1. I pointed this out to George and, no kidding, his eyes shone like struck matches. I was so proud that he was my kid. That look told you everything you needed to know about him.

Matches on Boxing Day are supposed to be special. It's football with a bit of magic in its boots. We're all full up on moping about the house and forced bonhomie and we want something real, something with some whack about it. Thankfully this is what we got: a cracking good game. We twice took the lead, firstly through Craig Dawson who, a few days later, was voted Coca-Cola League Two player of the month for December. The second goal was via a fantastic shot by Kallum Higginbotham but Crewe pegged us back to make it a 2–2 draw. While it meant we had lost a little ground to the clubs chasing us, the game was so enthralling no one seemed to mind. Another bonus for the 1,192 Rochdale supporters in attendance was that we heard the chant of the year, a brilliant twist on an old favourite. As Jason Taylor and Jason Kennedy warmed up, a special tribute was paid to our strawberry blond midfielders: 'There's only two ginger Jasons, two ginger Jasons.'

A couple of days later Morecambe visited Spotland and Dale made it seven wins in eight matches with a comfortable 4–1 victory. The winning habit was now truly installed and, quite rightly, Keith Hill was again voted as manager of the month.

January, 2010

A win looked likely away at Aldershot until they equalised three minutes before full-time. We returned to winning ways immediately, beating Cheltenham Town 4−1 at Whaddon Road with Chris O'Grady scoring a hat-trick. O'Grady had signed for the club from Oldham Athletic just a few days before on a two-and-a-half year deal, following his successful loan period.

That night, on the *Football League Show*, I recorded and played back the Dale goals repeatedly. It made me think how times had changed. Coverage of Rochdale used to be minimal, with practically no national profile outside of appearing in the league tables in newspapers and in the results round-up on television on Saturday afternoon. The *Rochdale Observer* was the primary source of news about the club and I remember how bizarre it seemed when Clubcall was set up, generating news from Spotland on a daily basis (Clubcall was a phone-line which fans could ring to hear pre-recorded interviews with the manager or players). Before then, Rochdale AFC appeared to exist on a match-by-match basis only. These days, across websites, Sky Sports, Radio Five Live and newspaper football supplements, we were featured extensively. We were no longer an obscure cult. As I hit the rewind button for the 20th time to see Dale's goals followed by Manish Bhasin pointing to the league table (which showed us nine points clear of Bournemouth) I realised how lucky we were to be enjoying success during such a media age. When, for example, Lincoln City walked Division Four back in 1975/76 (scoring 111 goals, winning 21 of 23 home

28

matches, drawing the other two), the feat probably merited a quick acknowledgement during *On the Ball* and a piece in *Shoot!* And that was it.

Port Vale came to Spotland and, the same as Accrington Stanley before them, 'did a job'. Word had clearly got round that we played a passing game and the way to counteract it was to break up the play, close us down. Vale did this extremely well and as we saw their players celebrate leaving with a point we realised once more the newfound respect the team had earned. We were more used to clubs treating us disdainfully, playing expansive football and fully expecting to leave Spotland with three points. We were 10 points clear of Bournemouth in second place.

After the game, I came home to an e-mail from Dinah Hill, wife of Benny, who we had visited in August: 'Dear Mark, the news has probably already reached you via the football grapevines, but just in case ... I should tell you that Benny died at home yesterday. As you know, he'd been failing for some time and was most frustrated and disappointed at not being able to do the things he wanted to do (including going with you to THAT museum). His passing was pain free and quite gentle, for which we have to be thankful. It could have been very different, as we'd been warned, with a ruptured aneurysm.' Benny was 82. We had spoken of visiting the Football Museum in Preston; he was a true historian of the game.

The news everyone had expected arrived at the end of January when it was revealed that Will Buckley was to leave the club. He signed for Watford who had made, Chairman Dunphy revealed, a 'good offer' for him. While we were sad to see him go, he had proved injury prone through the season and played only a small part in the team's success. He was the only Dale player with blistering pace but his final ball and goalscoring needed improving.

No one cried into their beer for too long in the Studds bar and most agreed that if it helped secure the long-term viability of the club, it was a decision that had to be made.

February, 2010

Over the last few years matches against Bury have become a little over-heated. Reports had leaked through to us Daleys that the Shakers were planning to pelt us with golf balls, potatoes with razor blades in them and restaurant-issue refrigerators. I didn't fancy that, and I didn't fancy being jeered at by hundreds of Bury fans telling us we were top of the league but had fucked it up or were having a laugh. Also, the match was to be screened live by Sky. We stayed at home. I'd made the right decision again. Bury won 1−0 and moved up to third place. Before they scored, Chris O'Grady missed an open goal inches from the line. This was shown over and over again on Sky to incredulous shrieks from the commentator. Those of us in the know had a good idea why he missed. Just out of shot but playing a crucial role was our non-friend Efe Sodje, another, much the same as Lee Hughes of Notts County, that fans of lower league clubs dislike on an almost innate basis (though the bandana and cow-boy-cocky walk doesn't help). As usual, Sodje was pulling and pushing his man, so although prodding a ball six inches in the direction in which you are travelling looks easy, it isn't if you've got a very muscular and determined Nigerian international (nine caps, one goal — I've checked) on your back.

Away from the television cameras Rochdale rediscovered their form in the home games against Crewe Alexandra and Dagenham and Redbridge, winning 2−0 and 3−1 respectively. Chris O'Grady scored in both games and further cemented his partnership with Chris Dagnall. While others had been tried out and largely failed in previous seasons (Jon Shaw, Lee Thorpe etc), Rochdale now had an authentic target man in O'Grady. Legs like sawn-off telegraph poles, O'Grady's forte was holding up the ball and bringing others into play. His technique sometimes seemed barely legal — basically pinning his marker down with a combination of arm, midriff and thigh but few referees penalised him for this manoeuvre. Most often, Big Chris would play the ball to Little Chris (Dagnall) and the pair would skip merrily through defences towards goal. Incidentally, Dale fans wondered whether Hill had a plan to bring players of the same name together in various parts of the field. We'd had two Wills on the wing (Buckley and Atkinson), two Chris's upfront and our ginger Jasons chasing everything down in midfield.

Our superlative display at Bradford City in December had clearly stuck firmly in the memory of their supporters. They were now 18th in the division and had replaced Stuart McCall with Peter Taylor as manager in a bid to salvage what was left of the season. Their web messageboards were teeming with grand prophecies. The consensus seemed to be that Rochdale would score at least five. So afraid were they that only a few hundred made the trip to Spotland. The Rochdale public, still largely ignorant of their table-topping team, didn't show up either, meaning the attendance was a measly 3,055. We didn't hit the dream football of December 1st and didn't score five. We scored one and they scored three and fully deserved their victory. It was only our second defeat in 15 games, the disappointment being that both losses were against local rivals.

I had been to Macclesfield Town's Moss Rose ground several times and it had been a pretty miserable experience. They were another ex-non League club that housed away supporters on an uncovered open terrace. The few seats they supplied offered no vantage point, so it was impossible to see much beyond shins and boots and tufts of grass. I had spied their Main Stand covetously on my visits there and saw that it was tall and positioned roughly half way along the pitch, therefore providing a perfect view. I had a plan. We were going to go in there. It was Macclesfield Town, after all, a family club, and both me and George weren't effusive types; we could contain ourselves for 90 minutes.

I briefed George as if we were on an army mission: no club colours, act normal, if we score go for a surreptitiously clenched fist rather than a throaty roar. We were doing great. Through the turnstiles, no problem. Past the steward at the bottom of the stairs leading to the seats. We were supposed to wave a ticket at him but because I marched in so sure of myself, he let me pass. He stopped George who, showing a commendable capacity for subterfuge, told him I had both tickets. I was, by then, so far up the stand that he would have looked extremely petty shouting me back: we were in.

The first half was bloody awful, typical lower league hoofing and chasing. At half-time, still successfully under-cover, we had a Flight Lieutenant Andy 'Mac' MacDonald moment. George was desperate for a pee but we weren't sure where the toilets were. In a moment of unforgivable laxity, very similar to MacDonald's (played in *The Great Escape* by Gordon Jackson) as he boarded the train that would have taken him away from Colditz, George asked a steward to direct him to the toilet, thereby revealing himself as, at best, a newcomer to Moss Rose and, most likely, a Rochdale fan. Luckily, George was pointed to the toilet without suspicion.

We scored a fortuitous goal and won 1–0. Afterwards their manager, Keith Alexander, well known for his prickly opinions, commented that, 'It's no wonder Rochdale are at the top of the league when they have that kind of luck.' Four days later, Alexander, aged 53, died after complaining of feeling unwell on the way back from seeing his Macclesfield side lose 1–0 at Notts County. He had suffered a brain aneurysm seven years earlier.

March, 2010

To boo or not to boo. We've responded in different ways to returning players at Spotland down the years. It was noted that David Perkins and Rickie Lambert had not celebrated their goals against us, for Chesterfield and Bristol Rovers respectively. It was also noted that when Grant Holt scored for Shrewsbury Town (albeit a stunning goal) he rolled about on the floor like a five-year-old overfed on worming tablets. I don't think it offended anyone but it didn't draw forth much admiration either. Before the match with Rotherham United, Adam Le Fondre spoke warmly of his time at Rochdale while stating — as footballers are duty bound — that Rotherham now paid his wages and he'd be doing his utmost for his new team against his old team. In the event, it was a non-issue. He barely touched the ball. Rochdale cruised to a 4–0 win and apart from the unexpected margin of victory the only slight shock was that Craig Dawson received his first booking of the season, when he fouled Le Fondre. To put this into perspective, if we were to take another centre half, say a local one playing in the same division, a Nigerian International perhaps, well, by the end of March 2010, Headband Efe had 12 yellow cards.

Our next visitors, Lincoln City, paid us the utmost respect and came with a one-track mind: a draw at all costs. Clearly we were now viewed as the (drum roll, please...) Manchester United of our division. Teams were refusing to engage in open football for fear of a spanking. Lincoln sat that famous 'two banks of four' across the pitch in the hope of suffocating the game. It worked extremely well and when they scored on a rare breakaway mid-way through the first-half, it meant they had a lead to protect. Chris Dagnall equalised but the Lincoln players still gave one another high fives as they left the field. Since when had a draw at Rochdale been marked so joyously? Things were looking up.

Shrewsbury is generally regarded as one of the best away trips of the season. The journey down is through pleasant country-side and handsome villages, and the club is renowned for giving visitors a warm welcome. I had last visited a few years earlier and it formed a nature trip as much as a sporting outing. We watched kingfishers darting across the River Severn before the match and afterwards made our way through chest-high Himalayan balsam as we followed a stream that ran directly behind the car park at Gay Meadow. Alas, Shrewsbury are Gay no more and have relocated to the Prostar Stadium, a newly-built facility on the outskirts of town.

We were warned beforehand that there was no parking for away fans and that admission was all-ticket. How welcoming! What a PR disaster: come to Shrewsbury, but there's nowhere to park and you're going to face the rigmarole of buying tick-ets when you get here. It's probably not the club's fault but is all down to sub-section 17, clause 5 of the local councils' act (1975). Still, when lower league teams are desperate for punters it doesn't augur well. Belligerent to the end, I figured it wasn't possible that there would be *nowhere* to park. I'm resourceful, quick-thinking: bound to find somewhere to dump the car. I was wrong. The choice is this: garden centre car park with warnings threatening clamping; ramping it up on the hard shoulder of a dual carriageway or abandoning it on a housing estate with 'residents only' signs fastened to every lamp-post. After much up and downing of the main road outside the ground (and we all know how that feels on a warm day with kick-off time approaching) I finally settled on paying £5 and leaving it parked up behind a petrol station, about a mile from the ground. Stupid bloody Shrewsbury. Surely they could have afforded to buy another farmer's field to accommodate parking for away fans when they built the new stadium.

Inside the ground I bought a bottle of water but was told I had to undo the top and leave the lid at the kiosk. I asked the lad why.

"Safety," he said.

"What does that mean?" I asked.

He shrugged. So, then, I'm allowed to leave the kiosk carrying a plastic bottle that weighs, say, half a pound but I can't have the lid with it, weighing a couple of ounces. Back at my seat I saw liquid running down the stands at various points where bottles without lids had been knocked over by people trying to manoeuvre in tiny spaces while carrying pies, programmes, scarves and coats. Strange world.

We won 1–0, although the scoreline flattered Shrewsbury who barely touched the ball. Afterwards, on the drive home, we tuned in to *BBC Radio Shropshire*. The next hour was probably the most blissful I have spent as a Rochdale fan. Numerous callers rang in, chiefly complaining about Shrewsbury's ineptitude but also praising Rochdale. Amid the acclaim was a delicious edge: if Rochdale can do it with such limited resources, why can't we—with our bigger and better ground, larger fan base? The joy was in the transition. We weren't being looked down upon but looked up to, used as a measure of what other clubs could achieve. They weren't saying we'd done it by financial trickery or sudden cash input but via the 'proper' route: developing a good squad, having a game plan. Much of your life as a football supporter is spent looking behind you at the previous game or forward to the next but right there in the car as the sun set on an early spring day, I was of the moment. I knew how wonderful it felt to be exalted and respected by other teams' fans and that it was a rare thing.

Further proof that we had players the envy of other clubs arrived a few days later when Craig Dawson was voted *FourFourTwo* magazine's League Two player of the season. Usually, this award went to strikers or midfielders so for Craig to win it was even more impressive. We felt ourselves lucky to have seen his first season as a professional; it was one of the privileges of supporting a lower league club. Apart from his ability, he was a Rochdale lad and played the game the right way, never scything down strikers or acting petulantly. By the end of the season he would pick up just one booking and score 11 goals, remarkable statistics for a centre back.

Another trip to a former non-League club loomed: Accrington Stanley. We managed to secure 'seats' but they were pressed so tight to the perimeter wall, I had to watch the game turned at an angle. I was so close to Tom Kennedy that I thought he might be tempted to pass the ball to me at several points. We were within sight of the Accrington 'ultras' and they were as good to watch as the game itself. They have a wide repertoire of songs and are a set of fans who don't sing only when they're winning.

Accrington took a two-goal lead but almost as if affronted by the cheek of it, Rochdale stormed back and won 4−2. Kallum Higginbotham scored the final goal from just inside Stanley's half. As the ball looped into the air and began to drop, the crowd shared a special moment. All fell quiet and there was still silence when the ball hit the net; people didn't believe what they had seen. A mass celebration ensued on the pitch with Frank Fielding charging out of his goal to join in. We each recognised that we had seen something special and — there and then — knew it would form a highlight of a very special season. As Dale played out the final few seconds of the game, the Ultras sang a song that we'd never had directed at us before: 'Where were you when you were shit?' They obviously weren't aware that it formed a backhanded compliment. The Daleys smiled broadly. The league table backed up the assertion too — we were 11 points clear at the top. We're not shit anymore!

While most people had noticed that Dale were having an unusually good season, the news seemingly hadn't reached Grimsby. Second from bottom, having won just five games out of 37, they must have considered a match against Rochdale more winnable than others because the board of directors agreed to lay on free coaches for supporters. Rochdale won 4–1 with Chris Dagnall scoring a hat-trick, his third in Dale colours.

April, 2010

I had given up on the routine should-I-or-shouldn't-I deliber-
ation before attending away games. Hell, this was a bona fide
promotion run-in and I was going to be at every game and take
whatever came my way firmly on the chin, smack. Such was the
enthusiasm, I packed the whole family into the car for the trip
to Chesterfield.

As we travelled along the motorway we suddenly lost speed
and could hear a clicking sound from the engine. I pulled on to
the hard shoulder. While we waited for the arrival of the RAC
man, I was (without telling anyone) weighing up the options. I
sensed that the car was knackered which meant we could either
all travel back with the tow-truck or, perhaps, maybe, possibly,
split the party with the diehard Daleys among us travelling on,
somehow, to Chesterfield.

I resolved to defer the decision until I had received some ex-
pert local insight from our RAC man. He confirmed, to be fair,
that the car was kaput, to be fair, and that to drive it a mile or
so further would result in us needing a brand new engine, to be
fair. He really did say 'to be fair' after every sentence, as if he'd
been a footballer in a previous life. I half expected him to say,
to be fair, that if it were his car he would not be over the moon
but in his job he had to take every call-out as it came. He told
us we were about 20 minutes from Chesterfield and the cost of
a taxi there would be about £8. I imparted this information to
the occupants of the car and the two lesser-supporting Daleys
magnanimously volunteered to accompany the tow-truck back

home while the two greater-supporting Daleys (George and me) travelled on.

The kindly RAC man drove us to a packed pub and said there was a special telephone on the bar permanently connected to a taxi rank. There wasn't. Still, I found a poster on the wall advertising a taxi firm and jabbed in its numbers. The taxi soon turned up and we clambered in. I started to explain to the driver what had happened. I got to the bit about us being 20 minutes away from Chesterfield and my expecting a fare of about £8 when he turned to face me, open-mouthed.

"You're fucking joking, buddy," he said.

He told us we were an hour away and the cost would be about £30. He pointed at the meter:

"Look, we're nearly at six quid already."

As he said this, I noticed we were passing the motorway junction where our car lay stranded. Our dim-witted RAC man had taken us about three miles in the wrong direction to drop us off at that pub. I wondered: was he really thick or did he get a kick out of passing on misinformation, jamming maximum hurt into an already-failing day? Should I ever see him again I may test out the tolerance of his forehead against a fast-running fan belt, to be unfair.

If I still believed in the FGs (Football Gods) and had not forsaken them at Bradford City I would have been able to make a perfect prediction of the day-to-come at Chesterfield. We would lose, maybe 2–0, to a couple of dodgy penalties scored by their lump of wood, Barry Conlon (see Julian Alsop, Cheltenham Town), and then we'd face an arduous journey home, taking perhaps four hours or so. All this came true but with a couple more added miseries — we rushed to Chesterfield Station to find we'd missed a connecting train, meaning we had to wait an hour, and we were jeered at by drunken Bury fans on their way home from a 5–0 defeat at Notts County. The whole day had cost me (petrol, taxi fare, match admission, half-time grub, train fare) almost £130. It must be love. Oh, and repairing the car cost £300.

That night I did a stupid thing: I looked at the Chesterfield websites. I don't know why I do this — the message posters are often spiteful. They were criticising Rochdale for not bringing many fans and not getting behind the team. We had taken about 1,000 but this was apparently no match on what they would take away if they were 'runaway' leaders. Everyone has a unique relationship with their club, forged over many years, and devotion or otherwise depends largely on how much it has been reciprocated. Chesterfield have had a reasonable amount of success in the past 40 years with cup runs and promotions — how dare they pass judgement on us as supporters when we have had so little in comparison. And as for getting behind the team, this was difficult when they stuck us in an open end. In fact, some of them thought it funny to warn us before the game: 'Bring your brollies.' Over the years I have being prepared to take the jokes and digs at Rochdale, the team and the club, but I'm touchy when it is turned on supporters.

Another thread on Chesterfield's messageboard was devoted to their fans being disappointed with Rochdale, not able to understand what all the fuss was about (the universal praise for the football we played). It was further evidence of the intensity of expectations that came with being top of the league. It clearly wasn't enough to have shown, by virtue of our league position, that we were, at that point, the best team in the league — we had to show it week after week; people had to see it with their own eyes. In truth, we had not been at our best at Chesterfield but they had got lucky with some erratic refereeing decisions and an inspired performance by Tommy Lee in goal. In a bid to match their level of peevishness I wished upon Chesterfield all the worst for their next game, away at Barnet on Easter Monday. They lost 3–1. As my younger son used to say to my oldest whenever he was told off for pulling a sneaky trick (such as stealing a biscuit off his 3-year-old brother): '*Deserves you right.*'

Bournemouth, despite an embargo on new signings and being unable to use loan players except in exceptional circumstances, had managed to hold on to an automatic promotion spot all season. Their fans had also made a great deal of various injury crises that had sometimes left them unable to name a full quota of seven substitutes. Across the media this had led Bournemouth to be portrayed as plucky underdogs with all the usual calls upon sympathy and admiration this might engender. To the better informed, their holding on to a top spot was merely further evidence of how much finance had been spent or saved to spend later on wages during the period before entering administration. Surely a club truly on its knees would be playing 16-year-old kids and getting hammered every week.

Typically, they were welcomed to Spotland on Easter Monday with chants of 'We're top of the league and we pay our bills'. It is perhaps difficult for fans of other clubs to appreciate how much of a badge of pride it is that we have avoided the serious turmoil that has led other clubs to resort to financial chicanery. We have become fanatical about this moral standpoint because it has, so far, been unimpeachable. We haven't won anything or done very much but we have gone about our business honourably. It is, however, unfair that we direct these chants — or messages if we're visiting other clubs' forums — to fellow supporters because they are not themselves culpable. They, like us, have to trust that the people who are left at the football club when we all go home, run it in on a decent and ethical basis. If they don't, it is the fans who remain to sort out the mess, raise the funds, and put up with jibes from the pious masses of the Spotland faithful.

The game ended goal-less and fans booed the referee Carl Boyeson (who had been one of those refs about whom both sets of fans warn: 'I wouldn't be surprised at any decision he makes in this game.') from the pitch. *Radio Manchester's* reporter misconstrued this as being directed at Keith Hill. By the time the match highlights (all 10 seconds of it) were shown on the *Football League Show* later that night the BBC bloke with an annoyingly posh and authoritative voice interspersed the 'commentary' with news that Keith Hill had labelled some of the Rochdale supporters 'sad' for booing his team off the field. How fast non-news travels. In the same programme, they made great play of how Notts County were catching us up in the league table. They were now seven points behind with a game in hand and due to play us at Meadow Lane in two weeks. Luke Rogers had warned the previous week that they were 'gunning for the top spot'. The thought of lovely Luke and his over-inflated look-alike, the lovely Lee (Hughes) on our trail was enough to make anyone run. Very fast.

While we had drawn with Bournemouth, Rotherham United, in fourth place, had lost, which meant that although we'd had a disappointing Easter, we were still 14 points clear in an automatic play-off place with most teams around us having just six games left, while we had seven. We needed five more points to be absolutely sure of promotion although three points in our next game might be enough, should other teams lose.

It had been a long, dark winter. Devon in the springtime was calling. We decided to make it a family break and spend three days in Torquay, taking in the match on Saturday afternoon. As we drove in, approaching the seafront felt as if we'd gone through a portal to another world. Trees were in leaf. The sunlight sent tiger stripes against buildings. It was clearly a looked-after town — no litter on the pavements, walls freshly painted in pastel colours, no tracts of wasteland where houses and shops had once stood. I thought of home, of Rochdale, the mess of it all. And how lucky people were to live in towns like this with a beach and the sea too, and sunset-red cliffs fringed by palm trees.

On Friday we walked from the hotel to the village of Cockington with its pink-walled thatched cottages. The sun set the skin tingling. We put our coats over our arms. A horse and carriage trundled by down one of the narrow lanes. We wandered into Cockington Church. I didn't pray for a Dale win; it seemed crass. Besides, we didn't need help from above; we were going to be fine. In the walled garden we sat down on a bench. The bees from a nearby hive were coming to life, still drowsy after their long winter sleep. They circled us lazily. A couple entered the garden and I saw that the man was a fellow Dale fan, Trevor Lorimer. He had been a stalwart of the supporters' club for many years. We chatted. He said he had seen numerous Rochdale fans milling around Torquay. I asked if he'd ever seen us play at Torquay before. He had.

"It slated it down all day and we played them in a night match," he said. "Must have been about 1975. We lost 1–0. Bill Summerscales scored an own goal."

I was suddenly there: back to 1975, a folded-over programme (costing 5p) in my snorkel jacket pocket; getting the 463 bus to Spotland; watching these figures flit across a muddy pitch; getting on the bus afterwards, the windows steaming up and me scraping out a port-hole so I could see if I was nearly home. I imagined that particular game against Torquay, too: big burly

Bill accidentally jabbing his toes against the ball and it flying past Mick Poole. All that way to lose 1–0. In the bloody rain. *All that way*. Trevor (then a young man, just starting out at the bank where he worked for years) and a few of his good-hearted, good-natured mates at the crush barriers behind the goal. There would only be 30 or 40 of them, a half-full coach-load, already considering the long journey home, mile after mile down an empty motorway, past fields and towns, feeling annoyed and stupid for trusting a team of no-hopers to win (or draw even) and make you happy. Thankfully, all that was gone now. This team wasn't that team. This team was a good team, a very good team. At the top of the league, looking down. If 1975 was the start of the journey, this was the end. We were going to secure promotion tomorrow. The scruffy, rained upon people of Rochdale were going to skip down these litterless, pastel-shaded streets. Tomorrow, this town, all this handsomeness, would belong to us. We deserved it.

We got to the ground early. I saw Jimmy Mushgrave, another Dale devotee. We had played together for the same junior team as kids. We shook hands.

"They're all here," he said, pointing to the ground.

I knew that by this he meant lads from school, mums and dads, grandads, lads who'd moved away to Cornwall and London or elsewhere but had converged on this patch of land about a mile from the edge of the sea. Outside the ground an impromptu game was taking place: Rochdale v Torquay United, all ages invited. It was moving to witness this spectacle and realise that, for once, things had truly, measurably got better. Football fans weren't fighting each other any more. They were playing together, having fun. Blue shirts were everywhere. Trevor had guessed that a 1,000 might come down but we learned later that it was almost 1,500. Everyone was heading to the sun.

Rochdale made a lively start, passing the ball well. There wasn't any penetration in their play but I guessed this would come later. I had seen them do this many times over the season — passing it sideways mainly but tiring their opponents before driving forward and scoring, often late in the game when runs were no longer covered. Torquay broke away and scored. Soon after they scored another. And another. At half-time we were losing 3–0, and stunned.

We were sitting down, separated by a wire fence and a handful of stewards from the home fans, who were mainly old folk. I looked across and one of these was standing up making gestures, holding up three fingers to indicate the score. He was pointing to his face imitating the frowns we were wearing and then holding his stomach as if laughing uproariously. I have never in my many years as a football fan been drawn into a confrontation with a rival supporter or wished harm upon anyone inside a football ground. At that moment, however, watching this buffoon acting like this in front of a set of Dale fans comprising mainly women, children and old-timers, I wanted to push my way past the stewards and chin him, good and hard. Instead, I did what all decent people do who have faith in the system and believe goodness will prevail: I complained. The steward said he would 'keep an eye on him' and I returned to my seat, recognising the futility of my complaint.

We had twice come back from 3–0 down before to draw, at Morecambe and Luton Town, earlier in the season and we told each other it might happen again. Then again, it might not. Torquay continued to play brilliantly and scored twice more. They also missed several chances and the consensus was that we were lucky they hadn't made it eight or nine. Every time they scored, a group of fans in the stand opposite ran towards the Dale fans, mocking and jeering. I couldn't understand this.

When my team scores my instinct is to celebrate with my own and grab the nearest person to me, all the better if it is a family member.

Back at the hotel, I was inconsolable. Most of the teams around us had dropped points. A win would have clinched promotion. Across football at that moment we were a laughing stock. Torquay, third from bottom, had beaten the league leaders 5–0 and we'd not had an excuse of having three players sent off or our two goalies hospitalised. Five and nil, fair and square, they had hammered us. The texts began arriving: 'What's going on?'; 'Huh?' and, best of all, 'Christ!' Where, through the season, we had been noticed for our unlikely and fantastic wins, we were now news because we'd been stuffed.

I had thought we were through with humiliation; this really hurt and dented my confidence in the team. I hadn't seen Rochdale so comprehensively picked off for many years. It wasn't a fluke result, five chances and five goals, it was an annihilation: their team running past ours at will, our players unable to complete a five yard pass. It reminded me of hammerings we'd had back in the late-1970s, when teams were so much better than us that they hardly bothered to celebrate a goal. Rochdale had always been notorious travellers. On four occasions in our history we had gone through whole seasons without an away win. I had watched them through two of these, in 1977/78 and 1982/83.

When I returned home I received an e-mail from fellow writer and Rochdale fan, Trevor Hoyle. He knew why we had done so badly in Devon: 'It was the sun wot did it – our lads never seen it before. Ball of glowing gas in't sky. Bloody Fuckin Nora! Mam!!!!!'

At least we only had a few days until our next match, Darlington at home. Darlington were 14 points adrift at the bottom of the table. They had won twice away from home all season. If we couldn't beat those duffers, heaven help us.

The largest crowd of the season, 5,371, turned up to see Darlington run through. Boy, were they due a beating. Dale were set to go on the rampage after the ignominy of Torquay. As we expected, Rochdale were magnificent. They tore Darlington apart. Shots rained down on their goal. Darlington barely crossed the half-way line such was the ferocity of our attacks. Rochdale had 19 corners. The pressure was relentless, chances galore. On practically their only excursion into our half, Darlington scored. Rochdale lost 1–0.

Bizarrely, after the game we learned that despite the win Darlington had been relegated while results elsewhere now meant that only Rotherham could catch us and take an automatic promotion spot. They had to win all their four remaining games and we had to lose all ours. If just one of the numerous chances had crossed the line against Darlington we would have been promoted — as good as, since our goal difference was +37, compared to Rotherham's +5. We went home knackered, not just from the maths but from the tension of the Darlington game: at times it was almost unbearable, to have so much possession, to dominate so considerably, and yet lose.

Again, we didn't have to wait long for our next match: four days. Appropriately it was against Northampton Town, the team I had seen Rochdale play in my very first match at Spotland in October 1974. It was a sunny day. Again, more than 5,000 were at Spotland and some of the regulars around us were displaced by newcomers and wandered off looking for seats, muttering. We tore into Northampton as we had done Darlington. After a few missed chances and the referee turning down a blatant penalty, we finally scored for the first time in four matches. The ball dropped to Chris O'Grady who swivelled smartly and sent the ball crashing into the net. This act looked decidedly straightforward after all the twisted geometry of the previous games.

Soon after half-time we sensed that the team was happy with a 1–0 as they began to defend ever deeper. The ball was punted repeatedly into our penalty area but we held out. Fans ringed the pitch ready for the inevitable invasion. After four minutes of injury time (from a game where they had not been a single injury of note), the referee finally blew his whistle. I had long imagined how I would react at this point. I could see myself crying, screaming, hugging everyone in sight. I didn't do any of these. I picked up my programme and, with my dad and lads in tow, set off to join the others on the pitch. It was relief more than euphoria. I think the reaction would have been different at Torquay or against Darlington but, by now, the frustration and stress had eaten away at the purity of the joy. I wanted to be mad-happy, clenching my fists and bruising everyone with hugs but it didn't feel right. After all that wonderful football through the season, win on win, we'd collapsed over the line, just made it. It was as if, at the very end, the old Rochdale (an embodiment of fatalism, ineptitude and insecurity) had tapped the new Rochdale on the shoulder and warned: 'I'm not done with, yet.'

The players came out and waved from the Main Stand, dancing on the spot, holding one another up. Frank Fielding pretended to start typing at a laptop in the press box. Gary Jones had his baby daughter in his arms. Announcements were made but the pa system was so tinny and loud that no one could hear anything beyond an exuberant noise. The Stone Roses were played and then Oasis' *Wonderwall*. People tried to sing along but were impatient for the chorus. Bugger it, everyone started the chant we've been chanting for 36 years (and more): 'Da-yul, Da-yul.'

Text messages began to arrive on my mobile phone. Friends were imploring me to celebrate, to submit myself to some kind of bacchanalian orgy. I suppose we each have our own customs built around football support. Some go on their own, others with mates, some sup four or five pints of beer before they pass through a turnstile, some are quiet, others are loud. Mine has always been largely family-based: I went to Spotland with my dad and then when I had kids we took them along too. So, bearing in mind my travelling companions, it didn't lend itself to anything too reckless. Besides, out on the pitch with all these fellow Daleys, I realised how few of them I knew. We wear the colours, carry the love, but we're pretty much a disparate group, even at times like these when we appear to be one huge throng of brotherhood. I looked around in vain for kids like me who'd stuck with them over the years but couldn't see them. In the end, we drifted away and, at each step towards the car, I thought of how many times we'd made the same journey and it had just been an ordinary day, another match gone, while now we flowed with the juice of knowing we were the chosen ones, the promoted. How much lighter we were on our feet.

One of the questions Keith Hill was asked after the match was the obvious:

"Do you think you can catch Notts County?" (Our run of one win in five matches meant we were now one point behind them and they had a game in hand.)

Hill answered, probably without thinking:

"If *we* don't, the tax man will."

Rochdale fans—and most supporters in the country—chuckled, but over in Nottingham it was a poke in the eye for the County crew. They set about their messageboards with fury. The vitriol aimed at Hill was as strong as many had seen aimed at one individual within the game. Most just stopped short at calling on supporters to physically attack him. County's new owner, Ray Trew, mounted a charm campaign, pointing out that while they had exceeded the division's wage cap for a period, they were no longer doing so and, therefore, were trading within League regulations. While this appeased some, others pointed out that many points had been accrued (thus propelling County to the top of the league) while they had been operating outside League rules. Trew did not offer to surrender these points or even a portion of them commensurate with the percentage overspend they had made on their playing staff.

Hill's quip was mistimed considering Rochdale were to play County three days later; it served to agitate their supporters and further focused the players. The match was billed as the League Two championship decider. The maths didn't look good. Notts County were unbeaten in 13 games (11 of which they'd won) while, of our last five, we had lost three, drawn one, won one and scored a solitary goal.

I didn't want to travel all that way only to lose and be mocked by legions of County fans who considered Hill's and our stance to be unfounded and self-righteous. Also, and this was a far better reason, I couldn't bear the prospect of Lee Hughes scoring and doing *that* dance in front of us or indeed anywhere within our field of vision. The most placid of men have found their fists clenched and froth on their lips at the sight of barrel-chested Lee doing his martinet routine, a huge sneer across his face. We lost 1–0. Lee Hughes scored. He did the dance.

Football fans are as happy as the last game or, at best, the last few games. We have to force ourselves to adopt a wider perspective; it doesn't come naturally. This was a confounding time to be a Dale fan. We were being feted everywhere and given unprecedented coverage across the media, most of it respectful and free of the patronising tone that used to accompany all things Dale. And yet amid this acclaim our recent form was wretched. We'd now won once in six games and scored one goal in 540 minutes of football. Everyone I met offered congratulation (for promotion) and then, immediately afterwards, commiseration (for our current form). Some Dale fans were bullish, refusing to be diverted from their promotion joy and viewing the remaining games as quasi-friendlies. Others were perplexed and a little worried: if we were losing to teams such as Darlington, Torquay United and Hereford United in this division, what awaited us in the division above? Either way, it took lustre from the achievement of promotion. We had, over the course of the season, become accustomed to winning and the pride and respect it kindled. We were missing it, pining for it.

The blip, slump, call it what you will, continued away at Hereford United. Craig Dawson made a rare error when he failed to clear a through-ball and soon afterwards Hereford scored again when Chris O'Grady pulled at an opponent's shirt in the box. While, playing it strictly by the rules, it was an offence and therefore a penalty, it was a decision a referee could make almost every time the ball was pumped into the box. Gary Jones pulled a goal back but, once more, the game ran away from Dale. Notts County lost at Port Vale, so a Dale win would have seen us close in on the championship. Bournemouth's win at Burton Albion, however, meant we were now only two points above them. We had collected just four points from the last possible 28; if we had been in this form throughout the season we would have finished with fewer points than Darlington at the bottom of the division.

On Sunday 25 April Rochdale learned that three members of the squad had been named in the PFA League Two team of the season — Craig Dawson, Tom Kennedy and Gary Jones. It was the second successive year that Kennedy had been included. In previous years few Rochdale players had made the team, and certainly no more than one player per season. It was a good indicator of the club's progress.

Two days later, Rochdale's chance of becoming division champions ended when Notts County travelled to Darlington and won 5–0. County were now seven points clear of Dale with only two games remaining for each club. Across the websites, Dale fans were typically robust, suggesting we were rightful champions because of County's financial shenanigans. We were arguing and shouting (metaphorically) because we were hurting. The championship had been ours for so long and, no matter what excuses were proffered (County's greater assets, their 'cheating', our players becoming tired, us not having back-up strikers), we had been unprofessional and let it slip, not seen the job through.

At last, some intricate passing football with an end product — actually, three end products: three goals. I was watching Todmorden Sports Under 11s take on Greetland Goldstars Under 11s in the Calderdale League Cup-final at the Shay Stadium (as it is now called), home of Halifax Town. Our Alec was playing centre forward and had mastered that Alan Shearer just-about-legal technique of leaning into defenders, making some room for himself so he could lay the ball off to others. Three times he did this and Todmorden scored on each occasion to win 3–1. The kids' match finished at 3.20pm which meant if I got my foot down I could make the second half at Spotland where we were playing Burton Albion in the final home game of the season.

It's a bizarre feeling not being at Spotland while a match is in progress. I think this has happened maybe two or three times in my life; I have to be seriously ill not to rouse myself from my sick bed. Although the game was largely irrelevant, I still desperately wanted to be there. I wanted it to be 0–0 when I arrived (so I didn't miss a goal) and 3–0 (at least) when I left. The turnstiles were shut so I entered the ground through the reception area. I passed the dressing rooms and almost knocked over Chris Dunphy as I took a left turn into the Main Stand. Dad and George told me the game has followed the now-usual routine of plenty of Rochdale possession, a few chances, but no goals scored. No worries, I'm here now: let the goal avalanche begin.

Burton, who had not won in their previous seven games, took the lead when a hopeful punt towards our goal by Cleveland Taylor looped over the reinstated Kenny Arthur, hit the bar and rebounded off Kenny into the net. Four minutes later Burton scored again via the penalty spot after the referee ruled that Craig Dawson had fouled Steve Kabba. Chris O'Grady pulled one back with 11 minutes to go when he chipped the goal-keeper. Dale fans were robbed of that beautiful sight of ball hitting net when a Burton defender scooped it away as it crossed the line. Despite the defeat, it was announced that the players and back room staff would do a lap of honour after the game.

I don't know whether it was the pointless (and unrewarded) mad dash down the motorway or the poor current form, but I decided to leave before the 'celebrations'. I felt we'd already marked the promotion after the Northampton game. Bournemouth had now overtaken us and we were in third place. A poster on *RochdaleAFC.com* later summed up the mood: 'Only Rochdale could make promotion feel like a wake.'

The day after the match I received a text from a Rochdalian who, since he lives in London, can only get to one or two matches a season: 'Couldn't believe half the crowd left before the lap of honour yesterday.' I was perplexed, trying to make sense of my feelings. On one hand I was the epitome of loyalty (36 years!) but then was I not mean and fickle for being among the half of the crowd that exited before the end? I think up until the Torquay game I was approaching that state of caring too much, wanting it too much. And something happened that afternoon at the seaside, all that way from home. Every few seasons or so there is a match when we, the crowd, share an overwhelming collective response that goes beyond habitual support, the everyday winning and losing. Losing so over-whelmingly had provoked a mental and physical reaction; we felt tired to the point of a headachy hangover. We had trusted completely in the team that they would win and we had for-gotten to hold back, temper our emotions, which meant we hit the floor hard and flat. Repeatedly friends asked me to explain how a team that had been 14 points ahead at the top of the table were losing to the likes of Darlington, Burton Albion and Torquay United. They had that condescending smile on their faces, once more — or maybe I imagined it, for paranoia is the first cousin of passion. Either way, it was a different expression to the one I had grown accustomed to through the season, the one that suggested a certain reverence and newfound respect for my club.

As expected, Craig Dawson won most of the end-of-season awards. He picked up Player of the Season; Young Player of the Season; Most Improved Player of the Season and the SMAC [South Manchester and Cheshire supporters' club] Player of the Season. Other award winners were Chris O'Grady who won the Supporters Player of the Year (beating Dawson by one vote); Jason Kennedy who was Players' Player of the Season and Kallum Higginbotham who received the Frank Bishop Goal of the Season award for his long-range shot at Accrington Stanley.

May, 2010

The timing of the announcement of Hill and Flitcroft signing new two-year contracts was probably strategic. It was done early in May, presumably to allay the fears of any players who were reluctant to sign *their* contracts in case the management team had plans to move on. In the event, it still didn't stop several key players leaving the club.

The final piece of authentic football business was the closing game of the season away at Barnet. The home side were in a relegation scrap and, should Grimsby Town win their away game at Burton Albion, they needed points to avoid the drop. News filtered through to Underhill that Burton were winning comfortably but Barnet still attacked Rochdale forcefully. With one minute remaining, Albert Jarret scored for Barnet and the 716 Rochdale fans who had travelled to the outskirts of London were left disappointed again, witnessing their seventh defeat in nine matches. If Dale had held out for that final minute they would have finished runners-up to Notts County (albeit trailing by 11 points), but the defeat meant Bournemouth pipped us by a point. Still, Rochdale were nine points clear of Morecambe in fourth spot.

Star turn at the civic reception held at Rochdale Town Hall the next day was the Mayor, Councillor Keith Swift, who serenaded officials and fans with his own take on the Frank Sinatra standard, *My Kind of Team*. When it came to Hill's turn to speak, he smiled and said:

"This could only happen in Rochdale."

Two days later Hill learned that his fellow managers, the members of the League Management Association, had voted him manager-of-the-year for League Two. The club announced that it had sold a record number of season tickets for the forthcoming season — more than 1,000. The list of released players was short, containing only Kallum Higginbotham and Ciaran Toner, while Kenny Arthur was given a free transfer and signed for Grimsby Town.

The first player informing the club of his impending departure was Rory McArdle who revealed that he had signed for Aberdeen. He was quickly followed by Chris Dagnall who moved to Scunthorpe United on a three-year deal, Tom Kennedy who signed for the same length of time at Leicester City and Nathan Stanton who left for a two-year deal with Burton Albion. The club did not receive a transfer fee or compensation for any of these players. Each had seen their careers revitalised while at Rochdale. There was also speculation about Craig Dawson moving to Middlesbrough who had made a reported offer of £450,000, which was turned down by the Rochdale board.

If promotion was new to us, so was this — our best players cherry-picked by other clubs. Routinely we lost a player to a higher club maybe once a season, not in batches of four or five. I thought it peculiar: these players had worked so hard for promotion, understanding what it meant to the club, the fans and the town but would now play no part in the next stage. I was reminded again that while they play for the club, they play more for themselves.

Before the return for pre-season training, Hill managed to acquire four replacements: Joe Widdowson from Grimsby Town, Brian Barry-Murphy from Bury, Jack Redshaw from Manchester City and Josh Lillis on loan from Scunthorpe United. Apart from Lillis who had spent one game on loan to

Dale in 2009/10, none of the others were particularly known to supporters. Early in July, Hill also captured, again from Grimsby Town, Jean-Louis Akpa Akpro (no doubt he will always be known as 'the French lad'—Dale fans struggle with English names, such as Kevin Townson, who was always known as 'Townsend' and David Bayliss who my dad called 'Bayiss').

In truth, these signings did little to salve the loss of stalwarts McArdle, Dagnall, Kennedy and Stanton. While these were each good players, they were also considered intrinsically 'Rochdale'—embodying what the club was about. They were honest and hard working and we'd effectively seen them 'grow up' from raw promise to consummate professionals. Rochdale without Daggers and TK and big Rory and the irascible, pigeon-chested Nathan was hard to imagine—they have been our travelling companions to promotion these past three seasons. They will, in time, have legendary status bestowed upon them, from Deeplish to Norden, because these were among the men who took us to the place we have coveted for so very long.

I did ponder: was this the reward for promotion? Was this what it was all about? Would we have been better finishing fourth and missing out again but our squad remaining intact and set to spend several more seasons out-playing teams in League Two? I suppose it was nothing unusual. It happened to all teams who were successful at any level. By virtue of gaining promotion your best players were more visible. Presumably it was incremental and while you lost players in the short-term this was assuaged by the fact that the value of other players would increase to reflect Rochdale's new status, and players of a higher standard would now wish to join the club and play in League One. All the same, the departed players as good as represented the heart of the team that had secured promotion. We will effectively be starting the season with a new team; only four members of the side that sealed promotion against

Northampton in April will definitely be starting the new season at the club and as many as six players could be making their first appearance in a Rochdale shirt on the opening day against Hartlepool United at Spotland.

Throughout the summer, I was asked: how do you think you'll do in League One? Based on how the team had fared until the end of March, I would have predicted a comfortable mid-table finish. Up until that point we were demonstrably superior to every team in League Two. The poor run at the end of the season installed insecurity and doubt into Dale fans, no matter the bluster they affected. Some old-timers began muttering darkly about the last time we spent a season in a higher division, 1973/74, when we won just two games all season and the club was left so demoralised it was no exaggeration to say it took us almost two decades to recover.

Keith Hill stated in August 2010 that the club was one of the worst funded in League One and could not compete with the wages others were offering players. This is nothing new, of course. Rochdale have always struggled for funds. Once more, the onus is on Hill to build a squad; to make average players perform above themselves and with energy and heart; to form a gameplan that will harvest points. He's done it before and the consensus is that he can do it again.

In the stands we will rally, we always do. We will embrace the new players, make them welcome and aware of what it means to wear the blue shirt, how special is the privilege. No one is quite sure how we will cope at this higher level but to even have to consider this is a joy. Many of us thought we would be stuck in the quicksand of the basement division for ever. The 2009/10 season saw the spell broken, the curse lifted. And that, for now, is more than enough.

★

Towards the end of the season, *The Times*, which has long held an affection for the club, commissioned me to write a couple of pieces about Rochdale AFC.

SUN RISING AGAIN OVER LEAGUE TWO LEADERS ROCHDALE, THE CLUB THAT TIME FORGOT

The Times, Saturday 6 March, 2010

The landmarks leading to Spotland are comically ominous. On leaving the M62, fans pass a sewage works, a pub called The Cemetery Inn and then, after running parallel to a graveyard, they finally reach the ground.

It is a journey I have made every other Saturday since 1974 when I was knee high to a mill-worker and it cost 25p to see a bunch of thickset blokes in Stylo Matchmakers hacking away at a football, and each other. In all that time, match-on-match, year-on-year, I have felt to be one of the accursed, an extra in a long-running sporting re-make of *The Omen*. We — Rochdale fans of a certain age — consider ourselves branded: born to lose. The sewage works, the graveyards, the defeats, the disappoint-ments, it gets into your blood, becomes you.

During my 36 years as a supporter we have been stuck firmly in whatever name football's proprietors have resolved to call the bottom division of the Football League. In fact, so long is our tenure that some call it the 'Rochdale Division'. We have had only one promotion in our 103-year history, to the old Division Three in 1968/69. Amid the losses, relegation battles and ritual humiliation there have been few highlights. Until now.

Rochdale, should they beat Lincoln City today, could go 11 points clear at the top of Coca-Cola League Division Two, a position we have held for more than three months. We have a goal difference of plus 39, a figure bettered by only one professional club in England—Manchester United. Promotion, most likely as champions, is highly probable. Read that sentence again. And then look to the skies and yell: 'Take that!' True football fans—not the effete flower-pressers who 'follow' Chelsea, Man Utd et al, know full well to whom this address is aimed: the Football Gods or, for short, the FGs. These are the deities routinely blamed for anything that thwarts the smooth passage to success of our football clubs. The FGs are symbolic of the deeper neuroses of football fans stalked by pessimism and negativity.

I have always accepted as an incontestable truth that Rochdale AFC is cursed, that the FG's tyranny over us is absolute. History has shown this. It is in fans' faces: nothing of note, of beauty, happens here. But something strange has happened. At around Christmas time just gone, a fan posted on one of the club's websites that we were on course for promotion. Other posters admonished him immediately. He was told not to provoke the wrath of the FGs. His response was simple and heroic: 'To hell with the FGs, they've p★★★ed on us long enough.' This was our 'I'm Spartacus' moment. We got to our feet, swung our 'college style' scarves around our heads and disowned the fear, the fatalism, and the FGs. The terminally ill had woken up cured. Over in the dugout, our effervescent management team, Keith Hill and David Flitcroft, could be heard muttering, 'What took you so long?'

Indeed, since Hill and Flitcroft, two ex-Rochdale players, were appointed in December 2006 they have been constantly perplexed by the congenital cynicism of the average Rochdale fan. They've assembled a fine squad of players. They pass and move, score goals, win matches. So why the long faces? They are right to take this view, of course, but it has led to occasional spats with fans who have an instinctive sense of ownership of the club and, therefore, its dismal legacy.

Keith Hill, it has to be said, is a peculiar chap. He is twitchy in interviews, looking away from the camera. He smiles, he frowns, but you sense that his face is revealing little of his true thoughts. This week he made one of his occasional speeches on the official club website. The gist was that he is 'under appreci-ated' but the syntax was so convoluted and ambiguous that no one was quite sure what he meant. Most of us have learned to ignore Hill's tantrums and tautology. It is enough that he is there each Saturday in his best Oasis jacket, kicking at the shale, fiddling with his stop watch and arguing with the old gimmers in the Main Stand. We know him like we might a daft younger brother. Sure, he's fidgety and his big beating heart is plonked on his sleeve but, let's have it right, he knows what he's doing.

What he has done is build a team far superior than anything we have seen in 40 years, possibly in the club's history. They play 'proper' football, the ball on the ground, passed patiently and craftily until the break is on and the ball fed to either Chris O'Grady or Chris Dagnall to accomplish the kill. The side is often graced with two wingers and that rare thing in the modern game: hometown players. Joe Thompson and Craig Dawson, both Rochdale lads, are often seen with kit bags flung over their shoulders, walking from home to the ground. Dawson, the most promising player I have ever seen at Spotland, has been linked with numerous clubs. The list of scouts at

Tuesday's 4–0 home win against Rotherham United stretched to more than 40 and most will have been appraising this 19-year-old centre half who has scored 11 goals already this season. He was a fan of the club as a boy and rumours have circulated that he signed a contract extension as an act of magnanimity: he wants the club to receive a transfer fee when he moves on.*

While Hill has justly received praise for the reinvention of the club, a crucial figure happy in the shadows has been club chairman, Chris Dunphy. A lifelong fan and board member for several decades, he has had the difficult job of straddling the old and new Rochdale, prudence versus progression, consolidation versus speculation. Hill has had frequent grumbles but he has been well served by Dunphy. The squad is huge by Rochdale's standards — back in the 1970s we started one season with 10 professionals. The only player we lost in the January transfer window was striker Will Buckley, to Watford. The club also has a wealth of costly support staff: dieticians, fitness coaches, sports scientists and a kit man, Jack Northover, who is slapped lovingly around the head by Flitcroft every time Rochdale score, which has been 69 times in the league this season. Pass the Nurofen.

Unfortunately the wider population of Rochdale has been slow to embrace its table-topping football club. The average attendance is just below 3,000 and it is unlikely that this figure will increase significantly, even with promotion. The town is on its knees and many people can't afford the indulgence of attending a football match. It is also a bloody mess. The cotton industry collapsed finally through the 1980s and 1990s and the recession has seen off what was left of any social prosperity.

* Sadly, Dale fans' affection for Dawson was tempered when he twice put in transfer requests in the close season.

When I was at school in Rochdale in the 1970s, we were groomed for either the mills or an engineering works. As these shut, kids were sent to work on industrial estates, loading lorries (the boys) or filing (the girls). Now these workplaces have gone too and old-boys in 10-bob uniforms wander around with torches, providing 'security' for non-existing firms. More than three-quarters of the people living in the Central and Falinge districts of Rochdale are on benefits, the highest proportion in England and Wales. Large swaths of wasteland are everywhere. Wooden boards have been erected to hide the blight; some have written upon them the lie: 'Rochdale is booming.' Buildings have been abandoned. The chain stores left town, replaced by pound shops. The *Rochdale Observer* — itself no longer based here — is a litany of wretchedness: 'Koran teacher jailed for sex attack on boy', 'Girl thug ruined my life', 'Four quizzed over murder'.

We hold on to hope, of course, and cherish the little stabs of handsomeness: the wonderful Victorian gothic town hall; the former library building now housing a local history museum; the rough moorland that frames much of the town; and, most of all, the football club. To go up that hill to Spotland and see fine football played by a good team is to be lifted above the mess and the misery. And it is also a pleasure to be among your own. We moan, we worry, we're cynical, but each of us is loyal, each of us subscribes to the club motto of 'Believe in the Sign'. It's been a long slog and we've lost some committed souls along the way but the new conviction, forged this season (promotion or not) — and forgive us our vanity here– is that good things do happen to good people.

Roll of Dishonour

Fewest wins in a season: two, 1973/74.
Lowest post-war Football League attendance: 588,
    v Cambridge United, 5 February 1973.
Most goals conceded in a season: 135, 1931–32.
Finished bottom of Football League: six times.
Attendances below 1,000: 31 occasions.

Famous Rochdalians

Grace Fields (singer/actress)
Sir Cyril Smith (MP)
Anna Friel (actress)
Lisa Stansfield (singer)
Bill Oddie (naturalist/television presenter)
Andy Kershaw (DJ)

Claim to fame

Rochdale is the birthplace of the Co-operative movement.
Joy Division recorded the track *Atmosphere* at Cargo Studios,
Rochdale, in November 1979.
Dunlop Mill, built from 14 million Accrington bricks, was
thought to be the largest mill in the world. More than 3,000
people worked there.
In 1915 Rochdale was listed as the most polluted town in
England.
The DJ John Peel worked at Rochdale's Townhead Mill for
six months in 1959.

AFTER YEARS DOWN HILL,
IT'S UP 'DALE

The Times, Monday 19 April, 2010

Misty night, October 1974. I'm 10 years old and we've just moved to Rochdale. My dad, 32 years old, fit and healthy, suggests we go and watch the local football team. It's a ramshackle ground full of ramshackle people, coughing and moaning. But when Rochdale score they stab the air and smile at one another, letting out this sound that is half-moan, half-roar: 'Daaaaaayyyyyyul.'

I want some more of this. I'm there for the next match, and the one after. If dad can't make it, I'm with pals from school. I wear the scarves and badges. I buy the match programmes. I learn the rituals. When we're winning we clap fast and it's a rhythmic 'Up the Dale, up the Dale'. If we're struggling it's a heartfelt and urgent entreaty: 'C'mon the Dale.'

I'm there all season, every season, 36 seasons. The ground changes around us, becoming bigger and smarter. The world changes and so do the people we sit with and stand among. Skinny kids from school put on weight and turn into blokes. Tough lads who used to lead the singing in the Sandy Lane End are now in the Main Stand, eschewing bovver for Bovril. Some of the old-boys have died. All that remains the same is the division in which we play. Matches against Lincoln City and Darlington etc come round ad nauseam as if on a carousel.

Suddenly, click of the fingers, it's a sunny day, April, 2010.

I'm 45 years old and finally, mercifully, we've been promoted. After the home win against Northampton Town there is the inevitable mad charge on to the pitch. My dad is now 67 and his arthritic knee makes it difficult to scale the perimeter fence. My two lads, aged 13 and 11, race back into the stands to help him. Walking across the Spotland turf, I go placidly amid the noise and haste. Perhaps the wait has been too long, the weight of history too heavy. It is not euphoria I feel but relief. Now, we can become a 'normal' football club, one that is not forever inert, jammed in the same division playing the same teams in perpetuity. I want to visit different towns and grounds, to stretch the horizon of my sporting imagination.

As much as I love my club, the muck and grit of failure is on my skin. I am bitter and I don't want to be. This team, I know, is the best I have seen and they have played slick, passing football all season, never resorting to the rough-house big-boot football of many of their opponents. But for so long I have seen others wearing the same shirts and many of them have been inept. You don't quickly forget finishing bottom of the Football League, 4–1 losses against Telford United in the cup or an 8–0 mauling by Leyton Orient. It becomes you. Maybe I just need time to adapt, to do what my football club has done: reinvent myself.

Back home later, I see that we are big news. The celebrations are shown repeatedly on television. On the websites, supporters of other clubs are wishing us well. A fan of local rivals, Bury, even summons qualified magnanimity: 'We'll miss you, you tramps.' I sense that people are rooting for us — and always have been — because we've never given up, never cheated, always believed. None of us Daleys wanted this job, 36 years at the bottom, the sufferers' sufferers. It's been unpleasant and it's been embarrassing. To many Dale fans, Saturday, this weekend, has been everything. I feel we've merely broken a spell, gone through a portal to a different place where, hereafter and ever more, it's going to be much more fun than whence we came. It was dark down there.

★

Happy talk.

Praise for Rochdale from fans of other clubs,
as posted on their forums.

Accrington Stanley

'Rochdale were some of the best fans I've seen at the Crown this season, as well as being the best team.'

'Higgy's goal was better than Beckham's if you ask me. It was on the bounce and in horrible conditions. Higginbotham was simply brilliant when he came on, ran rings round us.'

Aldershot Town

'O'Grady and Dagnall seemed to have a telepathic connection.'

Bournemouth

'The game was dominated by Rochdale for 80 of the 90 minutes. The three up front, Thompson, Dagnall and O'Grady were outstanding for them, moving at speed, peeling off each other and working every gap and channel.'

'The rest of the game was played out to a chorus of 'Oles' from the Dale contingent as their side knocked the ball about like Barcelona.'

'Credit to Rochdale who play football the right way and have a front three well worth watching.'

'Rochdale are by far the best team we have seen down here this season.'

'Rochdale were the far better team. If they play like that for rest of season, they'll win this league.'

'Hate to say it but once defeat was inevitable I really enjoyed watching their forwards play. O'Grady was awesome as a target — mobile, strong. Buzzy forwards like Dagnall, he reminds me of Le Fondre, are the only ones that cause Pearce problems.'

'Rochdale were an awesome side and played sublime football.'

'I couldn't believe the football that was played yesterday! It was fantastic, all on the floor, running at us with confidence.'

Bradford City

'If you finish above Rochdale, you will be automatically promoted.'

'They are the benchmark from what I've seen so far. Bournemouth might be a bit more solid and physical and grind out results but Rochdale have got a really decent team.'

'I think tonight I witnessed possibly the best team to visit Valley Parade in years. Looks like that is the standard set for all teams looking to get out of this division. Were so much better than Bournemouth. If Rochdale don't win the league then something has gone drastically wrong. And before all the Stuart bashers get their bandwagon going — hold your hands up and know that tonight we were done by a much, much better side than us.'

'Let's face it — Rochdale were awesome last night. They won the game in the first 25 minutes with some high tempo, stylish attacking football, and with constant pressure, two men at a time, whenever we got the ball. We made errors, yes. In tennis they would be called enforced errors. By far the best team seen at Valley Parade this season, and they deservedly go top.'

'Dale were simply stunning, the best team I've seen at Valley Parade in the last two seasons, never mind this one.'

'I can categorically tell you that Rochdale are the best League Two team I have ever seen, as their demolition job at our place showed.'

'Rochdale are quite simply a cut above EVERYBODY else as no other team have made us look so poor.'

Burton Albion

'I expected us to lose today. Rochdale are an extremely good team, probably the best team I have seen this season (alongside Torquay perhaps). They will finish in the top seven for sure.'

'Early goal silenced the away fans who came in impressive numbers. Well done to those Dale fans that made the trip to Pirelli Stadium today, nice and loud. Some fans that come don't sing much but you joined in today.'

'Well done to Rochdale. Best team I've seen this season.'

'Cheers to Dale fans for coming in droves!'

'I am not kidding, I thought to myself half way through the first half that Rochdale are playing in the wrong league. They are definitely League One material.'

Bury

'I've been a big fan of Rochdale and the way they play football. They are a team of energy, aggression and have decent technical players.'

'You deserved it [the 3–0 win at Spotland]. Should have been more, really. Three wasn't too bad as it could have been about five or six.'

Dagenham and Redbridge
'Dagnall and O'Grady are probably one of the best strike forces about at this level.'
'I'm yet to see a better team than them this season.'

Lincoln City
'Men against boys is the right description.'
'I think it's great for them and their supporters to have such a great team after all the years they have suffered like us. They must surely win the league unless something goes dramatically wrong. Good luck to them.'
'Rochdale are the outstanding side in the division this season. Their goalscoring capabilities are frightening.'

Luton Town
'Everything you'd expect from the best team in the division above us. They didn't show us anything that we didn't expect. I thought we were great, they were excellent.'

Rotherham United
'Well done Rochdale, they ARE the best team in the league.'

Shrewsbury Town
'Quite simply shown how to play football by a team far and away the best in the league.'
'In my mind Rochdale have been one of the best footballing sides in this division for the past three or so years. Always enjoy games with them, as you know you will see a well-organised, good footballing side who can mix it when required. When they play, there will always be one decent team on the field.'
'On the plus side, it was a pleasure to watch Rochdale!'

Torquay United

'We've played a very good side today and I think we need to give Rochdale credit. They were an absolute handful up front.'

'One of the most embarrassing days as a Torquay fan, today. We were a complete shambles from start to finish and to come away with a 2—1 defeat was daylight robbery. It should have been five or six on the balance of play. Rochdale were taking the piss and we didn't manage a shot on target until the game was over.'

PART TWO

And Other Football Stories

I

Interviews

Paul Moulden — Barry Hines — Stuart Hall — Colin Bell
Richard Jobson — Mike Doyle — Colin Bell (reprise)
Tommy Gore

★

CHIP SHOP LAST STOP FOR THE ULTIMATE PRODIGY

The Times, Monday 14 October, 1996

Footballers, because they are invariably young and extremely fit, are bathed in light. Their skin shines. They move swiftly. They exude life. Paul Moulden still carries this halo of effervescence. He also has the inventory of a footballer's life — the house in the suburbs, a modern dress sense and a frank, cordial manner: a footballer likes to get along with everyone.

Unfortunately, football and Paul Moulden have not been getting on at all well. Since leaving Manchester City in 1989 he has fallen down the leagues with stop-offs at Huddersfield Town, Rochdale and Accrington Stanley. Now, for the first time since he was 10 years old, his Saturdays are his own. It has been a hell of a journey.

Others have endured the ignominy of this down-escalator but few are former England schoolboy and youth internationals or have had their goalscoring prowess registered in *The Guinness Book of Records*. Perhaps most poignant is Moulden's age. He has just turned 29, no age at all in the modern game.

Moulden was the ultimate sporting prodigy. During the 1981/82 season, when he was 15, he scored 289 goals in 40 games for Bolton Lads Club, an astonishing average of 7.2 per game.

"People sometimes joke that we must have played the blind school every week but we were just a really, really good side," he said. "We beat the junior teams of clubs like Rangers with players who later became pros."

In six seasons with Bolton Lads, Moulden was never on the losing side. Two of his team-mates also graduated to the professional game—Julian Darby with Bolton Wanderers and Ian Scott with Manchester City. At 16, Moulden also joined City, a goalscoring legend before his professional career had begun.

The goals continued. He was top scorer for the reserves during the 1984/85 and 1985/86 seasons. On New Year's Day, 1986, he finally made his Football League debut, an episode tinged by farce. Moulden believed he had travelled to Aston Villa to make up the numbers. Billy McNeill, the City manager, had a peculiar way of announcing the team. Players not selected would receive chips with their pre-match meal. Moulden's arrived without chips. He was in. During the match there was a portent of a career to come. He was put through on goal with a five-yard start on Paul Elliott.

Moulden said:

"He caught me up. Paul was quick but I realised I didn't have the pace. I'm fast over a few yards and my brain works quickly enough but really I should have seen it then and there ..."

Despite a healthy return of 18 goals in 64 games for City, Moulden was not considered an authentic first-teamer. McNeill left to be replaced by Mel Machin who, in football vernacular, didn't 'fancy' him. He was the first of several to feel that way.

"I've learnt that you can't really persuade a manager to change his mind once it's made," he said. "I play as I do and I've got confidence in myself but I remember Mel always saying he was trying out some new system and whatever it was, it didn't include me."

He signed for Bournemouth and after a season with them returned to the North West to join Oldham Athletic. Moulden conceded that Joe Royle, the Oldham manager, 'did not realise how slow I was'. He was sold to Birmingham City where Terry Cooper was happy for Moulden to play his natural game. Barry Fry, Cooper's successor as Birmingham manager, was not enamoured, preferring his strikers to be faster, bigger and more aggressive.

"He did not have the lightning pace that's needed these days," said Lil Fuccillo, Fry's assistant. "He trained hard and was a good lad but he'd lost what pace he might have had. If he'd been around a few years earlier, he would have had a long career in top-class football but times have changed."

There lies the downfall of Paul Moulden. He is an anachronism: a player built for a different era. He is, unashamedly, a goal-poacher, delighted to prod a toe at a deflection and see it hit the net. He will not push and shove, trail a defender down the touchline or drop back as a quasi-midfield player. Players such as Moulden, though often coveted by fans, are seen as a luxury in the modern game. Their area of expertise is too narrow.

"I was looking for someone who was more of an athlete," said Machin. "His goalscoring record speaks for itself but the game is so quick these days. Having said that, I am surprised he's now in non-League football. It seems a waste."

Royle also feels that Moulden has slipped prematurely out of the professional game.

"I bought him as a back-up striker and when I played him he often scored," he said. "He was a very hard worker but I felt he ran with the ball too much and he could have been a yard quicker. I would have still thought he was talented enough to have had a longer career."

Moulden finished his professional career at Rochdale in May, released by Mick Docherty for, Moulden claims, refusing to carry out an explicit brief to 'get his arms up and crunch people'. Moulden's subsequent decision to quit was born not from bitterness but a pragmatic acceptance that he had to find a life beyond the game.

"Football's been great to me," he said. "I've been all over the world, seen things other people dream of. But you've got to get on with your life, a proper life that is, at some point, and now seems like the right time."

He has bought a chip shop close to Burnden Park in Bolton and is determined to make the business a success.

"It's the best thing I've done in the past few years," he said. "I'm working hard at it, doing 12 hours a day and, unlike football, it stands and falls on my own efforts, though Clare [his wife] and my mum and dad have been a great help."

Until a few weeks ago he was still playing. He signed for Accrington Stanley in the UniBond League. After being left out of the squad for a match with Lancaster City, he resigned.

"We got a new manager and he was another who didn't fancy me. That's the way it goes, isn't it?" he sighed. And then, smiling, he adds: "I have been asked to train with another non-league team and an agent from Scotland has been chasing me."

His skin is still shining.

* Paul made a success of his chip shop and still runs it. He has three young sons and coaches at Bolton Lads Clubs and works with youngsters at Manchester City's Academy.

KES, SWEET BIRD OF
BARNSLEY YOUTH

The Times, Saturday 9 February 1998

The wind and the mud; the PE teacher with thighs like beer barrels and a voice like bloody hell; the scrawny, pencil-thin kids using their shirt cuffs as handkerchiefs; goose pimples and chattering teeth — we've all been there.

It was August in Barnsley and the sun should have been warming their backs but a chill wind chuckled vindictively across the playing fields of St Helen's Secondary Modern School. The crew were constantly offering their extras — local schoolchildren — hot drinks, but in their hearts they knew that every shiver, grimace and bored expression was film gold.

The schoolboy footballers in *Kes* were playing for England, the picture of England drawn by Barry Hines in his book *A Kestrel for a Knave*, on which the film was based. Mr Sugden, the PE teacher played unforgettably by the late Brian Glover, decreed that it was Manchester United versus Spurs in a fifth round cup-tie but it was a far more important encounter. It was the disillusioned versus the disadvantaged, the bully versus the bullied. What chance had they when Sugden was both Bobby Charlton ("I'm scheming this morning, all over the field") *and* the referee? In the course of the most infamous games lesson in British history, Hines used football as the consummate metaphor of life. Billy Casper, the book's protagonist, is a dreamy, downtrodden waif in borrowed shorts. He is made the scapegoat when 'Manchester United' lose 4–3. Afterwards, he is imprisoned in the showers and Sugden slyly moves the temperature gauge to its lowest setting.

"He'll get pneumonia," Casper's classmates plead.

"I don't care what he gets," snaps Sugden.

Suddenly, Casper appears at the top of the partition wall. He has climbed free and is greeted by laughter; an away win for the disadvantaged.

Football has seldom transferred well on to the page or screen. Hines is one of a handful of writers with an innate ability to present the sport without the schmaltz. To him football is a reflection of the lives from which it offers a fleeting respite. It is a slog against cheats and bullies, kickers and cloggers, and the last man standing tall can claim a victory of sorts.

Hines was introduced to the game by his grandfather, John Hines, a gifted local footballer. While he was growing up in the mining village of Hoyland Common near Barnsley and earning praise for his own footballing ability, Hines was told constantly: 'Tha'll never be as good as tha grandfather.'

He applied himself better than his grandfather, who was, according to Hines, 'a bit of a wide boy' and played for the junior teams of both Barnsley and Wolverhampton Wanderers, before being selected to play for England grammar schools against Scotland in 1957.

While studying physical education at Loughborough Training College, Hines wrote the draft of his first novel, *The Blinder*. Brian Glanville had earlier published *The Rise of Gerry Logan*, widely regarded as the first authentic football novel. Before these, there had been two types of football books — works of fiction that were fanciful and superficial and others on a theme of 'My Life in Football' whereby old pros would bolster their pension plan by putting their names to a bloodless autobiography.

The Blinder, published in 1966 when Hines was 27, takes the reader inside the dressing room, where the clank-clanking of studs resonates and the language is as strong as the tackles out on the pitch. Word filtered through to Hines several years ago that a former professional had read the book and commented, 'Whoever wrote that book knows about football.' It is a compliment he holds dear.

"I see the book now as crude but it has a lot of vitality. When you are young and full of it, that is the type of book you write," he said.

He became absorbed into the culture of football by both playing the game and watching Barnsley.

"There used to be four of us who went to Oakwell. We'd get there about an hour and a half before the kick-off. As soon as they opened the turnstiles we would rush down the terraces to stand directly behind the goal. I don't know why we always ran because we'd be the only ones in there anyway at that time."

During one match he noticed a football stud near the perimeter fence, priceless treasure to a youngster. He hurried over and scooped it up.

"I got home and my dad said, 'What have you got that for?' I said it might have belonged to a Barnsley player, maybe Skinner Normanton or Jimmy Baxter but he just didn't understand. I remember being upset by his response."

Hines writes his books and television dramas in a tiny office on the campus of Sheffield Hallam University where he is an honorary Fellow. A line of postcards, most of them miniatures of famous paintings, adorns a shelf. Otherwise it is spartan, save for a kettle designed to hold enough water to fill a single cup. He does not have a word processor and writes his material in pen before passing it on to be typed. He volunteers that he does not drive, nor own a video recorder.

"It's madness, I know. We've got a telly but we've had that for about 20 years and it's only a small one."

He is lithe and his movements quick and precise. When the words run out he springs from his chair. "And he would turn his back like this ... " For a second he is Tony Currie and then Denis Law, dancing beyond imaginary defenders in this small, dark room. He sits back down and reflects, aware once more of his surroundings. His personality is very much like his writing — matter-of-fact, unadorned. As in his books, he can sometimes seem to drift away, suspended in his own thoughts. A smile is imprinted across his face when he recalls Barnsley's promotion to the FA Carling Premiership. In his work, he often invokes the occasional dash of otherworldly magic as a counterpoint to the relentless itchy realism. Barnsley in the top division still holds this sense of magic for Hines, nearly 10 months after promotion was secured.

"It is absolutely wondrous," he said. "I never imagined them in the top division. I can remember when they were in the old fourth."

He is not a frequent visitor to Oakwell these days and — better whisper this in Barnsley — often lends his support to Sheffield United. In mitigation, he proffers that he now lives in Sheffield and has a son who is a Blades fanatic.

"I saw Barnsley at Bramall Lane a few years ago and it was a strange experience. They were wearing blue and it didn't seem too bad but when I see Barnsley in red I feel all the old pride coming back. It's like first love, isn't it?"

While Barnsley found themselves adopted by a clutch of celebrities at the end of last season, Hines preferred to court the shadows:

"I would have felt like a carpet bagger after all this time."

For him football is too important and too enmeshed in people's lives for half-measures. While his club loyalties are divided, the football man within him remains steadfast.

LOOK ON MY WORDS
AND DESPAIR

The Times, Saturday 24 April, 1999

Gold watch, gold buttons, gold skin. The voice drips gold too, a molten flow of singsong syntax. The R's roll richly, the C's are clipped curtly and we are told of rutting stags, yaks, snowflakes and, of course, Ozymandias, king of kings. The match ended as a draw, incidentally. As if we cared. Stuart Hall is in town and everyone knows it.

"Joe, Joe Royle," he shouts as the Manchester City manager gets out of his car. The waiting press corps want a quote about one of City's new signings. Stuart Hall wants Joe Royle. Stuart Hall gets Joe Royle.

"You're late," admonishes Hall and issues the famous hee-hee, ho-ho chuckle. This small chap in a smart suit leads Royle, a large pallid man in a washed-out tracksuit, to his office. Hall is about to interview Royle for a radio station.

"Right Joe, the first thing I'm going to say will be along the lines: 'City were off the pace and crap for a while but now you're charging towards promotion. What's happened?' Something like that, anyway. Okay?"

"Fine," replies Royle.

Hall claps his hands, then rubs them together kindling an invisible flame with happiness, sheer bloody-minded happiness. Has Moss Side ever seen a sunnier morning? During the interview, Hall draws in close. His nimble fingers tug at Royle's clothing. He wants him to get the joke, share the joy. Royle, since he is a football man cut from granite and turf, does not reciprocate, but the smile reveals everything. He is thinking: 'This man is mad but I like him.' Hall will later say as much himself:

"I live in fantasy land. I have a following of fellow nutcases."

City is Hall's team.

"It's in my blood," he says. "I used to stand on the terraces as a boy with my father. I call Maine Road the theatre of base comedy."

A few years ago Martin Edwards, his tennis partner and ex-Manchester United chairman, encouraged him to buy shares in United.

"I said: 'Martin, I'm a City supporter, what are you talking about?'"

After his interview with Royle, Hall wants a cup of tea. He strides into the canteen at City's training ground. There is no one to be seen. Onwards to the kitchen. Through the swinging doors.

"Helloooo," he sings, "Helloooo?"

His father told him never to miss an opportunity and this has become a doctrine. Television, radio, corporate parties, business schemes — he doesn't so much run at life as knock it over, pin it to the ground and pose for the victory photograph.

"Everything I do I am enthusiastic about. If I'm bored with something I don't do it," he says.

Hall is 68 and looking good, not that he would agree. The dashes of gold, the tan and the beatific smile are man-made diversions. He has said before that he is not happy in his skin.

"I hate my body. I am runty, ill-formed, 5ft 8in and desperately wish I was 6ft-plus."

Later he will joke with our photographer and ask him to

superimpose some 'thick black hair' on to his head. Health-wise, a recent hospital check-up revealed that he had 'the heart of a 10-year-old and arteries like Bentley exhaust pipes'.

Every Saturday he brings a touch of Las Vegas to wet and windy football grounds in the north of England, from where he is asked by *Radio 5 Live* to file a match report. The station and its listeners know that 'match report' is a loose term. Extremely loose. His contemporaries tell us who passed to whom, who suffered a thigh strain, who scored the goal. Hall, in a voice as rich as fruit cake, mixes the profound with the absurd. His surreal monologues have become part of the nation's sporting fabric. The sentences are short and resonant.

"Snowflakes. Floating like a gauze. Past the floodlights. Ice, cold, vinegar. Hitting red hot steak and kidney pies. And fresh chips ... I just self-indulge. I make noises in my head. I like to entertain myself."

His father was a self-made millionaire in baking and confectionery. His Irish-born mother cluttered the home with books and he was encouraged to read the likes of George Bernard Shaw and Oscar Wilde, writers of great eloquence and wit. They have remained with him.

"We always bandied words around. My mother had a great gift for English," he says.

His expressive voice, more Gielgud than Motson, was nurtured at Glossop Grammar School where he played the piano and was taught to infuse his voice with the same rhythm and melody. He joined BBC Radio in 1959 and became a television presenter six years later on the magazine programme *North West Tonight*. He wore cardigans and sat in an easy chair 'to reflect the lives of the people and not talk down to them'.

He came to national prominence in 1966 with *It's a Knockout*, which ran for 16 years. His irresistible, out-to-lunch laughter was the delightful accompaniment to, among other things, 15 ft-high Styrofoam chickens toppling from rope bridges into over-sized paddling pools. It was Hall's inner world come to life. Millions visited this world on a weekly basis but in a moment of sniffiness, the BBC axed the programme. Hall did not sulk. He bought the rights and £500,000 worth of props. It is now a successful touring event; Microsoft has just booked it for a staff party. The chicken is still crossing the rope bridge.

Hall's life has not been without tragedy. His first son, Nicholas, died in his arms in a hospital waiting room when he was three. He had suffered a heart seizure.

"It was as if a black hole had opened up in my life," he says.

In 1989 he came close to bankruptcy as a Lloyd's 'name' when the financial crisis hit the insurance syndicates.

"I was frightened every time I heard the postman. I didn't know what the next letter would say. I nearly lost everything."

Two years later he was charged with shoplifting from his local Safeway. He was acquitted of stealing a jar of coffee and packet of sausages. During the case, a procession of Safeway staff— who might have been expected to tow the company line— spoke of their fondness for Hall. He had a word for everyone, he brightened their day.

"The girls were lovely for speaking up for me," he said after-wards.

There have also been several failed businesses.

"I've never been brilliant in business," he says. "If you have an artistic bent you're never going to be good at the logistics of business. I've no time for all that. I'm the man who ran Shit Travel—what a great venture that was." He is referring to Stuart Hall International Travel, the acronym from hell.

Hall has maintained the common touch. When he visits

Bolton Wanderers, for instance, he cherishes the reunion with the club's octogenarian tea ladies.

"They always say to me: 'Oh you look lovely today'. I say: 'I know'. 'Who got you ready?' they ask. 'Me mam,' I tell them." He laughs, and laughs some more. He is still giggling when we hit the street. A City fan passes on crutches.

"All right, lad?" Hall shouts.

"Not bad," he replies.

"Yes you are, you're on crutches!"

They both laugh. It feels momentarily like a politician's walkabout, except there are no votes to be had; our protagonist is doing it for fun.

"Why are you so popular, Stuart?" I ask.

"I don't know, I really don't know."

NOBILITY REIGNS IN THE COURT
OF KING COLIN

The Times, Saturday 9 January, 1999

Snorkel jacket pockets were stuffed full of them or else they were a blur in someone's hand as complex swaps were negotiated. Thin strips of pink chewing gum came with the cards and this gave them a fruity aroma, the sweet smell of youth.

Football cards were a schoolyard currency of their own. In Manchester, where I grew up, a City or United player was worth a small bag of conkers, unless they were George Best or Colin Bell. Then you were talking a Subbuteo team, a *Scorcher* annual *and* a bag of conkers.

Best and Bell were the antithesis of one another. Best was young, gifted and reckless. Bell was young and gifted. Their personalities were disparate, but, for different reasons, they personified a certain cool. On the field Bell was both flamboyant and industrious, a natural athlete who was graceful on the ball, tenacious without it. Away from the pitch he had a rare humility, a quiet dignity that is almost extinct in the modern game. During his 13 years as a player at Maine Road he helped win the first and second division championships; the FA Cup; the European Cup Winners' Cup; and two League Cups. He also collected 48 England caps after making his international debut as a 22-year-old. He played his last game for City 20 years ago, yet the mention of his name still draws heartfelt eulogies from supporters. He reminds them, of course, of a classic era in the club's history but also epitomises much more. He is perceived as being true to himself, devoid of ego and pretension. They call him 'King Colin' in the blue parts of Manchester.

I usually travel light — a notebook and a pen — but as I knock on the door of Bell's house I have a bag over my shoulder containing numerous photographs and football cards for him to autograph. Word has got around and I'm suddenly an emissary for every football fan I have met in the preceding few days.

"Colin Bell? You're going to meet Colin Bell?"

Soon, sun-stained and frayed posters from old *Shoot!* magazines are thrust before me:

"Please ask him to sign this ..."

The flowing, straw-coloured hair of his playing days has been replaced by a spiky cut. His labrador pounds into the hall and Bell wrestles it into another room. At 52, Bell is still lithe at just a few pounds over his playing weight. He seldom gives interviews, so he converses as he would at a bus stop or on a train, never resorting to formula or overwrought anecdotes.

John Bell, his father, worked from the age of 12 as a miner in their hometown of Hesleden, Durham. Bell's mother, Elizabeth, died soon after he was born and he was brought up by her sister, Ella. He is ambiguous about his mother's death.

"She went into hospital to have me but didn't come out again."

As a boy he was happy in his own company and spent hours playing football alone.

"I've never really needed close friends. I've always been a loner," he said. "I used to go on the green and play football all day. I'd sometimes throw a tennis ball on to a sloping roof just to practise heading or chesting as it came down. I never walked anywhere; I would always run. I had to be where I was going in the shortest possible time."

A clutch of clubs, including Arsenal, were interested in signing him but he chose Bury.

"I went there simply because they were the friendliest club. They had made me really welcome. I went for £12 a week but if anyone else had offered me £50 a week, I would still have gone to Bury." Bury were managed by Bob Stokoe, whose parents had moved to the town from the North East to be near their son.

"A few of the players used to go round to their house on Sunday night and play cards with them," said Bell. "Bob's mum would bake a cake and biscuits. It used to be the highlight of the week." He relates the story without acknowledging how downbeat and anachronistic it sounds.

He joined City in March 1966 when Joe Mercer and Malcolm Allison were building their classic City side.

"It was like a happy family. We couldn't wait to get into training in the morning. The ground was like a magnet. Joe did all the talking for the club and Malcolm did the graft with the players. He was a great motivator. You knew a lot of it was bull but after he'd spoken to you, you felt you were the best player in the world."

Allison, recognising Bell's extraordinary stamina, nicknamed him 'Nijinsky' after the famous racehorse. Exceptional performances, especially during the championship-winning season of 1967/68, inevitably brought fame and Bell was uncomfortable with it.

"I hated all of it. They wanted me to make records and all kinds of things. I didn't even like opening school fetes or signing autographs. I was okay with a ball at my feet but I don't like microphones."

His career effectively ended on a misty December evening in 1975 when he was just 29. City were playing Manchester

United in a League Cup fourth round tie when Dennis Tueart pushed the ball into Bell's path.

"The ball kept bobbling and I couldn't get it to sit right at my feet. I was aware of a player coming across towards me."

He recalls contemplating — in a split-second — several options but 'chose the wrong one of three'. He checked his run but was immediately 'clattered below the knee' by Martin Buchan, the United captain. His knee was bent back the wrong way at great force, tearing ligaments and rupturing blood vessels. City won 4–0 but according to legend many of their supporters left the ground in tears, sensing the gravity of the injury.

Bell did not play again for two years and among City fans there was a brooding resentment of Buchan. Bell, typically, has remained tactful about the incident:

"I hope it was an innocent challenge."

Did Buchan ever contact him to inquire about his wellbeing? He shakes his head. I ask Bell whether he would have done so if he had hurt another player to such a degree.

"If, in my own mind, I knew it was a complete accident, I would have done, yes."

He returned to the side at Christmas 1977, coming on as a substitute at half-time against Newcastle United when the score was 0–0.

"As I waited in the tunnel I could hear my name being mentioned all around the ground and everyone got to their feet when I appeared. I'm not an emotional person but I had a lump in my throat." City went on to win 4–0.

Bell played 35 more games though his injury restricted his movement. In the summer of 1979 he announced his retirement.

"Malcolm came to me and said he thought it was time I called it a day. He could see that I was fuddling my brain to work around the limited movement I had. I would have gone on forever and a day trying to get my leg okay but Malcolm was right, I'd given it long enough."

For a while he worked with City's young players but was laid off during Francis Lee's tenure as chairman. He says he would rather not discuss the issue; he feels that the club has had enough bad publicity in recent years. Under David Bernstein's chairmanship, however, he was invited back and is now employed in an 'ambassadorial role'. He attends supporters' functions and mixes with sponsors on match days.

It is possible to detect a tinge of regret that his role does not run deeper. He still exudes a deep love and knowledge of the game and he has the kindly, commonsense outlook of a football club's favourite uncle. City are at present on a purge of their backroom staff but there is surely a limit. Sign here Mr Bell; nobility will never go out of fashion.

SHELF LIFE BEYOND B&Q

The Times, Monday 8 September, 2003

Old footballers don't die. They go to B&Q. And they ponder: pine or mahogany shelving? Metal fixings or wooden? What am I doing here?

Richard Jobson had his first B&Q moment a few Saturdays ago. It was about 4pm and he found himself at the checkout. One or two people were taking surreptitious stares. He could read their minds: 'Isn't that thingy, you know, used to play for Oldham and Manchester City? Leeds too, I think.' Jobson paid up, loaded the car. On the way home (in the inevitable traffic jam) he realised the finality of it all: the footballer had become an ex-footballer.

At least he had delayed the inevitable. Until his retirement this summer, Jobson, at 40, was the oldest outfield player in the English game. Also, unlike many of his contemporaries facing civvy life or the volatile world of management, he has moved into that rare thing in football — a secure and steady job. He is chairman of the PFA and has joined its team of executives.

During a professional career lasting 21 years and spanning every division, Jobson played nearly 700 games for eight clubs. He made two appearances as an England B international and the various transfer fees totalled more than £1.5 million. These are the facts that will summarise his career in reference books but they make no hint of the cataclysmic changes that have coincided with his time in the game. Boom to bust, curly perms to chrome-domes, Jobson has seen the lot.

Today, players are picked up by Premier League clubs from about the age of 10 and nurtured meticulously. Few escape their watchful gaze to step up later from the lower divisions. In contrast Jobson played a handful of games for Burton Albion in the Northern Premier League before signing for Watford in 1982 when they were in the top flight.

"It was hard to take in really," he said. "I was only 19. I'd been playing in front of a few hundred at Burton and suddenly found myself on the bench at Anfield. We were 3–0 down at half-time and I was sure I was going to get put on. I'm glad I didn't because I was so nervous."

His starting wage at Watford was £150 a week, enough to convince him to abandon his degree in civil engineering at Nottingham University.

"The contract was just put in front of me and I signed it. Everyone did in those days," he said.

Graham Taylor, the Watford manager, used Jobson sparingly, prompting a move to his hometown club, Hull City, in 1985. Five years later he joined the Joe Royle-inspired revolution at Oldham Athletic. After Oldham's relegation from the Premier League, Jobson returned to the top division with Leeds United.

"Wages really started to spiral with the big Sky deal in 1995. The players became absolute superstars and football moved into another dimension," he said.

He rejoined Royle at his new club, Manchester City, in 1998 but was out for an entire season with a serious knee injury. Two specialists advised him to quit but another operated and said he could continue if he trained carefully and paid attention to his diet. Jobson also decided to quit drinking, a decision that would have been difficult earlier in his career.

"You'd often have a major piss-up after away games. One manager — I'm not naming him — would always stop off at a pub and make everyone have a drink, whether you wanted one or not."

Dropping down the leagues with Tranmere Rovers and, finally, Rochdale, his career ended ignominiously in May at Macclesfield's Moss Rose ground. He had not played in the previous eight matches but was told an hour before kick-off that he had been selected. Rochdale conceded two late goals to lose 3–2 and finish five places from the bottom of the Nationwide League. Jobson trudged off disconsolately with only one team-mate realising it was probably his last game and offering a hand-shake.

Despite the Rochdale manager's job twice becoming vacant during Jobson's spell at the club, he was not asked to apply. He was surprised but admits to being ambivalent about manage-ment.

"Some days I really fancy it and on others I wouldn't touch it with a barge pole," he said. "It takes over your life. The phone never stops ringing. You've got half the dressing room liking you and the other half hating your guts."

After announcing his retirement he set about patching up his body. He had another operation on his knee; one to remove cartilage from his nose; and a bridge containing six teeth was fitted to his upper gum.

"I've had so many elbows smashed into my face," he said. "I didn't bother to get my nose and teeth done until I'd packed in because it wasn't worth it."

His 15-year-old son, Ben, has also had a tooth fitted after it was knocked out playing rugby.

"Tubes of denture cream are all over the house!"

He first became a PFA delegate while at Hull and has been

chairman for two years. He must resign the position in a few weeks now he has finished playing. In the meantime he has started work as a full-time executive at the PFA's Manchester headquarters. He is still adapting to the role.

"You realise how lucky you have been as a footballer," he said. "You'd do a couple of hours training in the morning and be back home in no time. It was great being around the kids so much [he also has twin daughters, Alex and Olivia, aged 12] and having everything done for you."

Before he took up his new job last week, Jobson spent most of the summer with his wife, Sue, overseeing work on a barn they are converting in West Yorkshire, hence the trip to B&Q.

"I started to miss playing when the friendlies began," he said. "But then I remembered I went through it all last summer and wasn't picked for the first game and felt devastated."

Maybe 21 years is more than enough.

How times change ...

1982 : The only live televised football matches were the FA Cup Final and major England internationals.

2003 : Live tonight, take your pick from Dagenham and Redbridge Ladies v Macclesfield Town Matriarchs; Botswana Under 15s v Catholic Missionaries Over 65s; or Manchester United v Arsenal (again).

1982 : Watford, Jobson's first professional club, had one foreign player, Jan Lohman from Holland.

2003 : Their current squad (which is a good deal foreigner-light than most) boasts: two Jamaicans, an Australian, a Canadian, a Trinidad and Tobagan, an Icelander and an Englishman called Paolo Vernazza.

1982: Many clubs insisted players lived within 15 miles of their ground.
2003: It's a novelty if they're in the same country.

1982: Teams were allowed one substitute.
2003: Extra stands are being built at most clubs to accommodate the five subs, the reserve team, the Lucozade-throwers, the physiotherapists and the psychiatrists (who insist on a reclining bench).

1982: Players wore shorts that ran a serious risk of indecent exposure should they make a sliding, hmm, tackle.
2003: Shorts are back down to the knees. Diddy players often look like urchin extras from a street scene in *Oliver!*

IRON MIKE STILL PACKS A PUNCH

The Times, Monday 9 February, 2004

Eventually, the question has to be asked. He's got the shirt, the scarf, the legacy, but he needs to know: 'Dad, have City ever won anything? You know, apart from promotion from the odd division here and there?' Dad starts to think. Memories of Lee, Bell and Summerbee flash past. And matches against exotically named teams such as Gornik Zabrze; heart-stopping cup-winning goals from overhead kicks; the roar of the Kippax; a lump in the throat.

It seems like yesterday but it's nearly 30 years since Manchester City secured a prestigious trophy. The last City captain to lift silverware was Mike Doyle back in 1976 when they won the League Cup. Before that, over a few short years Doyle and Co had won the League Championship, FA Cup, European Cup Winners' Cup and the League Cup once again.

While others from that era provided flair and glamour, Doyle was the man for consistency and commitment, the absolute love of the shirt. Famously, he also defined himself as the hater-in-chief of the other lot, Manchester United. In fact, irascibility was — and still is — Doyle's business, his specialist subject. Whether it's his non-mates at Old Trafford or the doyens of his local golf club, stand well back: this may well smart.

"I just get on with life. I couldn't give two hoots what people say about me," he says.

Well, variously, they say he is obstreperous and arrogant, determined and honest, a little hot-headed too. Indeed, in his autobiography to be published soon, three separate 'chinnings' are detailed in the preamble alone. Later we learn of his desire to strangle George Best and of the lovingly tended bile aimed at Rodney Marsh. Finally, he tees one up for the golf club folk with whom he's recently had a fallout: 'They're ten-bob millionaires who are fuelled by jealousy and pettiness. They're back-stabbing no-marks with no lives of any substance.' Take that. And party.

What's it all about Mike, all this spleen, after all these years?

"I first did my autobiography in the 1970s but you couldn't swear in books back then and you had to be careful what you said about anyone. I take people as I find them and say what I think, if I'm asked."

He started his football career with this same philosophy, falling foul as a 15-year-old apprentice of Bert Trautmann, the City legend. He had teased the German goalkeeper after a heavy defeat and was cuffed around the ear. 'He was a cocky little bugger and needed taking down a peg. As a senior professional, I thought I deserved a little more respect', wrote Trautmann in *his* autobiography.

Doyle played his way into the City team at 18 on £7 a week and remained a permanent fixture for 16 years, making 572 appearances. He forged a special relationship with supporters because he was local-born and a boyhood City fan. More importantly, like many of them, he reviled Manchester United. This first surfaced publicly in the early 1970s when he announced:

"I can't fucking stand them, simple as that."

He suffered serious consequences. The tyres on his car were slashed. Windows were smashed at his home. Threats were made on his life and for a while he had police protection. He was only saying what he thought. He's still saying it today.

"United's support was built on sympathy after the Munich disaster. If you go to Old Trafford you don't see that many people from Manchester. I'll never understand why you get these knob-heads coming up on coaches from places like Torquay to support them. I went to one game and all I heard was Irish accents, hundreds of them."

Amazingly, he almost signed for United in 1972. A deal was agreed between the City and United managers at the time, Malcolm Allison and Frank O'Farrell, but it is believed the response from the City board was, 'Over our dead bodies'.

Doyle was a stalwart of the team under the reign of Joe Mercer and Allison and confirms the general view of their successful partnership. Mercer was the 'genial figurehead' while his younger assistant was the dynamic motivator. Doyle is damning about Allison's decision to bring Rodney Marsh to the club in March 1972 and disturb a settled, winning team.

"Rodney Marsh only ever really represented Rodney Marsh and everyone else could go and get stuffed as far as he was concerned," he says.

Is he surprised that Marsh has had a second career as a television pundit?

"No, all Cockneys are gobby, aren't they? He's done well out of portraying a false image."

While he played, Doyle had part-ownership of a garage business but on retiring from football he worked for Slazenger, supplying products to golf clubs. He was a fanatical golfer himself until 1999 when a chronic knee injury sustained during his football days meant that he could no longer play.

"It was like chopping my arm off being told I could no longer play," he says.

He fell into a deep depression and began drinking.

"I was round at the Late Shop as soon as it opened. I'd drink two litre bottles of whisky a day," he says. "My son, Grant, had to hide bottles from me. I wasn't staggering all over the place. It was more a case of wanting to be asleep."

In his book Doyle covers this two-year period with the same candour he reserves for other aspects of his life. His wife, Cheryl, left him briefly and he became estranged from Natalie, his eldest daughter, who is still not on speaking terms.

"We've weathered the storm and stuck two fingers up at the petty bastards who would have taken great delight in seeing me attempt to destroy myself and watch my family fall apart," he says.

Doyle cuts a curiously benign figure in the armchair at his home conducting the first of many interviews to promote his book. He's wearing slippers and has a crossword puzzle at his feet. He isn't suspicious or snide but defiantly honest and uncomplicated.

"Write what you like," he says.

At one point, Cheryl is a bit slow replenishing his cup of coffee and he tells her:

"Bloody hell, get a move on, will you?"

He still loves City and, like all their supporters, has looked on bemused at their fluctuating fortunes down the years. Talking to him, it's hard not to believe that the resolve, tetchiness and flinty charisma he personifies are essential to win football matches, and honours.

RELUCTANT HERO REVISITS
HIS PAST

The Times, Monday 10 October, 2005

The self-styled St Alan of St Annes got it wrong, very wrong, when he predicted the repercussions of England failing to beat Poland and qualify for the 1974 World Cup finals.

"It will be a terrible thing for six weeks and then everybody will forget about it," said Alan Hardaker, the autocratic secretary of the Football League. "It is a football match, not a war. Let us keep our sense of perspective. Everybody is getting hysterical."

He was in a tetchy mood because Sir Alf Ramsay, the England manager, had asked that the League fixtures be suspended the Saturday before the game, so he could better prepare the players.

Wednesday 17 October 1973 has never been forgotten.

"We absolutely paralysed them," said Colin Bell, a member of the England team that fateful night. "We laid siege to their goal but just couldn't create a winner."

ITV paid £50,000 to screen the match live and the nation, stricken by power cuts and three-day working weeks, invested its collective hope in a team that Sir Alf had cited as better than the World Cup winners of 1966.

"It was the most one-sided match I ever played in during my career. On any other night we would have won by five or more goals. We hit the post, the bar and defenders on the line," said Bell.

While the 1–1 draw meant England missed out on World Cup qualification, perhaps its greater damage was to the psyche of the players and supporters. It was impossible to believe sport could be so unjust, that 11 men could comprehensively outplay their opponents and not finish victors.

"Normally it took me two or three days to get over a bad result but it was three or four months later before I began to feel right in myself," said Bell. His wife, Marie, felt it had a profound effect.

"He was distraught. He didn't bring football home with him usually but he was so subdued. He walked around as if he was on a different planet."

Poland '73 is one of the topics Bell is asked to discuss repeatedly with fans and he returns to it again in his autobiography *Colin Bell – Reluctant Hero* (Mainstream Publishing, £15.99) to be published on October 20.

"It is one of those games that never seems to fade from memory. It's all been stirred up again with England playing Poland next week. I was in my prime at the time and the four years to wait until the next World Cup seemed a lifetime away."

Unfortunately, two years later his career was effectively finished when he suffered a serious knee injury. He was playing in a League Cup tie against Manchester United when a Martin Buchan tackle 'smacked' him on the knee. The full extent of the injury was not known until a few days later.

"My knee bent backwards, bursting blood vessels down my leg. All the ligaments in my knee were torn. I was told later that there had been a definite risk of thrombosis, which could have killed me. I never considered it at the time but they might have had to amputate the leg."

Although he tried valiantly to regain fitness, he had limited mobility and finally retired from the English game in 1979. Unknown to most fans, he spent the summer of 1980 with

San Jose Earthquakes, a franchise then owned by the current Portsmouth chairman, Milan Mandaric. One of his team-mates was George Best which meant the two players viewed by many as the most talismanic to have played for City and United sometimes roomed together.

"I found George easy to chat to and very down to earth. I never went out drinking with him. I was known for my stamina but I didn't have *that* much," jokes Bell.

Back in England he spent most of his time at the restaurant he established with Colin Waldron, the ex-Burnley defender. Bizarrely, the next summer, 1981, he was coaching youngsters at Butlin's holiday camps in places such as Bognor Regis and Skegness. A City fan had invited him along — he also found himself judging glamorous grannies competitions.

He returned to football proper in 1990, working with young players at his beloved City. The appointment of Neil McNab to the youth set-up and the bullish approach he instituted clashed with Bell's genial style.

"He treated the youngsters as if they were adults playing in the first team. I dreaded going into the club. I was deeply unhappy and didn't know what to do."

Eventually he made his feelings known to his former teammate Francis Lee who had taken over as City's chairman. Lee responded by sanctioning a new two-year contract for McNab. Frank Clark arrived soon afterwards as manager and one of his first actions was to dismiss Bell in a 'clinical and cold way' along with other members of the coaching staff, including McNab.

"I felt Francis Lee let my family and me down very badly," said Bell. "I didn't expect any favours but the manner in which I was treated was wrong."

A year later, with Lee and Clark themselves removed from office, Bell was invited back to the club in an ambassadorial role. Since then City supporters have petitioned for Bell to have his due recognition. He was voted their all-time best player and a stand at the City of Manchester Stadium bears his name. In 1999 he was selected as one of 100 best footballers of the 20th Century and in January of this year was awarded an MBE. He is soon to have an exhibition dedicated to him at City's museum.

This surge of interest prompted Bell to write his autobiography. Unusually for a footballer's memoir, it is enigmatically under-stated and written in much the same way Bell played — effectively but with great humility. The most telling anecdotes are found away from the game: Joe Corrigan, City's giant goal-keeper, carrying him downstairs at home after his devastating injury; the death of his mother when he was a baby and the subsequent tug-of-love between his aunt and father; his acute shyness as a boy that caused him to dread reading aloud in school.

"My favourite film is *Billy Elliot*. I couldn't believe it when I saw it; that could have been my story except it was football and not ballet. It was uncanny." Sometimes the quietest of blokes have the best stories to tell.

* The England v Poland game of 1973 was one of the first live televised matches I watched. I have seen thousands of games since but it still remains the most unjust score-line. I distinctly remember struggling to accept that a game could be so massively one-sided and yet a win wasn't guaranteed. The failure to qualify meant that during my childhood I was denied the opportunity of seeing England in the World Cup finals (they failed to qualify in 1978 as well as 1974). It meant I was 18 before I saw them make the later stages, in Spain '82. Just one more goal against Poland would have made the difference.

In the original piece *The Times* left out the paragraph about Colin Bell and George Best sharing a room. The sub-editor clearly hadn't grasped the significance: Bell and Best, legend and legend, in the same room, kipping. Imagine: 'Good night, Colin.' 'Good night, Bestie.'

GORE AND GLORY;
THE UNLIKELY HERO

The Times, Monday 13 August, 2005

Chelsea? No problem — been there, done them. Pele? Much the same. Tommy Gore may have missed out on football's riches but he is a man wealthy on memories, most of them forged in Wigan. In 1980, the midfield player, now 51, scored the winning goal at Stamford Bridge when Wigan Athletic played there in the third round of the FA Cup. He was rewarded handsomely — a £100 bonus and all the chips he could eat at the scruffiest Chinese restaurant in London.

Wigan were in the Fourth Division at the time. They had joined the Football League the previous season after making 35 applications for election. Chelsea, managed by World Cup hero Geoff Hurst, were going through a lean period, battling for promotion from the old Second Division with the likes of Tommy Langley, Clive Walker and Colin Pates in their team.

"They were still a big club, though," said Gore. "We noticed all the expensive cars parked up outside the ground."

In contrast Wigan were run by two full-time administration staff and another three looking after the players, one of whom was manager Ian McNeill.

"The facilities we had amounted to green grass and a ball," said Gore. "We trained on a field that was part of a public park. It didn't matter because the spirit in the club was fantastic."

After a spell as a youth player at Liverpool, Gore had joined

Wigan in January 1974 when the club were in the Northern Premier League. A few months later, while spending the summer playing for Dallas Tornadoes in the United States, he found himself marking Pele who was making his debut for New York Cosmos in a pre-season friendly.

"I was impressed most by his balance," said Gore. "He's not a big man but his strength is amazing. He just knocked our two centre backs out of the way."

At the end of the game Gore swapped shirts with the Brazilian; it is framed and mounted on the wall of his house in Billinge, near Wigan.

He remembers the cup-tie against Chelsea being in doubt because of icy weather.

"It was a terrible day, absolutely freezing cold," he said. "I suppose the slippy pitch was a leveller but we were a good team anyway and just gave it our best."

His goal came in the first-half when he lobbed Peter Borota, Chelsea's Yugoslavian goalkeeper.

"It broke on the edge of the penalty area and I hit it on the turn. It was purely instinctive."

Wigan held on to their lead, helped by the heroics of John Brown, their goalkeeper. Afterwards the team dispersed across London but Gore and Fred Eyre, the reserve team manager, could not find anywhere to celebrate.

"Everywhere we went was shut. We couldn't believe it," said Eyre. "We ended up in the scabbiest Chinese restaurant in London. I wouldn't walk through the door of a place like that now, never mind eat in it."

Eyre had taken most of the reserve team players to the match but the club had not been able to afford to put them up.

"We were sneaking them into our hotel," he said. "We had them on the floor, in the cupboards, anywhere we could."

In the next round Wigan lost 3–0 against Everton at Goodison Park in front of 54,000 supporters. Nevertheless, the board, without Dave Whelan at the time, marked the victory over Chelsea by treating the players to an end-of-season holiday in Spain.

"I remember we had to play against a team of waiters at the hotel because the club wanted to put the trip down as a business expense," said Gore.

After retiring because of injury at the age 30, Gore owned and ran a snooker club in the town for eight years. He now has a small company providing contractors for ships. He has watched Wigan's progress closely and is secretary of the past players' association.

"If you'd have told anyone back then what was going to happen to the club, they'd have got the men in white coats to take you away," he said. "Unbelievable isn't the word for it."

Does he rate their chances against Chelsea and for the rest of the season?

"They've got to have a go, give it their all. I've always considered myself privileged to have played in Wigan's first ever League game [a 1–1 draw away to Hereford United in August 1978] and the cup match at Chelsea was another turning point because it made us believe we could go anywhere and get a result. The current players have got to have that same attitude."

---

* The piece was run to preview Wigan's first game in the Premier League, against Chelsea. There were dire warnings that they would suffer routine humiliation against the better-funded sides. They lost 1–0 against the eventual champions to a goal by Hernan Crespo in the 90th minute. Wigan finished the season in 10th position, 16 points from the relegation zone.

2

Broken Idols

Jason Ross — Pedro Richards — Bobby Stokes
Gary Charles — Paul Gascoigne

★

I was commissioned to write a series of features looking at the darker and tragic sides of football. Before writing about sport I had covered 'hard' news for the newspapers where I worked, so I was no stranger to the 'death-knock'.

A TRAGIC LIFE WEIGHED DOWN BY EXPECTATION

The Times, Saturday 27 November, 1999

The metal shutters at A.J. & G. Wallman's Convenience Store are pulled down, even in daylight hours. The nearby doctors' surgery has bars at every window and a high fence on all sides. Collyhurst was once a thriving suburb of Manchester, with pubs, churches, families and hope. It is now a barren thorough-fare, a place to pass through quickly, eyes wide shut.

A small sign is chained to a lamp-post across the road from Wallman's. It reads: 'Accident Here, Can You Help?' Just a few hundred yards along is another sign: 'Chip Shop Open'. The prosaic and the profound are often neighbours.

The local paper called the accident a 'Horror Smash'. The terminology is routine but by any definition this was the real thing. A 22-year-old man had been leaning from the passenger window of a car driven by his best friend. He might have been waving to girls or cracking jokes at the expense of passers-by; either would have been typical. He was lost in the moment and did not see a parked car they were approaching. His head struck the vehicle and smashed through the rear window. He died soon afterwards in hospital; it might have been a blessing, such were his dreadful injuries.

In the days after the accident reporters covering the death of Jason Ross stumbled upon an unexpected angle. Jason was the son of Trevor Ross, a footballer who had played for Arsenal and Everton. He was also the grandson of William Ross who had worn the colours of various Scottish clubs before joining Bradford City in 1950. Jason Ross would have been a footballer too but life got in the way.

He was born in July 1977, a few weeks before his father made his full debut for Arsenal. It was soon apparent that Jason had the innate skill of his ancestors.

"It was there in him right from the start," says his father. "It just came natural for him to kick a football."

In childhood, as in later life, Jason was man-marked by disquiet.

"He was one of those kids who are always on the go. If he wanted to get from A to B and there was a brick wall there, he went through it. He never slept ... *never* slept," says his mother, Janet Mizon. "I remember crying through the night, thinking:

'What have I done to deserve this?' He could catnap for a couple of hours and then he was up again, running around, or playing football. We took him to see every consultant going. They used to sedate him for me. Nothing worked. I bet he was about five or six before he slept through a whole night."

Trevor Ross remembers Jason's early childhood differently. He says his son was 'no problem, no problem at all'. Trevor Ross and his ex-wife see many things differently, for the break-up of their marriage was prolonged and acrimonious. They separated nearly 14 years ago and desperately wanted to move on but their son's erratic life — and the complexities of why it should have been so — has acted like bindweed.

Jason remained with his father at first but later settled permanently with his mother and her new partner. It meant he was no longer around footballers and football clubs. Indeed, for long periods of his life he was out of contact with his father.

"Kids would give Jason photos of Trevor to sign," says Mrs Mizon. "He couldn't even get to speak to his dad for Christ's sake so how could he get him to sign anything? So he started telling lies. He'd forge it; do what ever they wanted. He got to live in this dream world."

During his teenage years Jason began stealing, usually from those closest to him.

"The police asked me whether I ever told him I loved him. 'All the time,' I told them," she says.

She felt Jason was pining for his father. Trevor Ross believes his ex-wife had turned Jason against him and made access difficult. He says he did see Jason sporadically but these visits had to be kept secret from his mother, who disapproved.

"I didn't desert Jason. He knew where I was living and the door was always open to him, but Jason was one of those people who would do what he wanted to do," he says.

Meanwhile, Jason excelled at football. He spent a season at Manchester United's School of Excellence. He was strong physically with an astute football brain. He joined Rochdale, believing he would have more opportunity at a lower league club.

"I'm convinced he would have made it in football. He was such a talented lad and the kind of lad you could take to," says Tom Nichol, Rochdale's former chief scout.

Jason was expected to make the first-team by the age of 18 but suffered a knee injury and was released from his contract. It provided a smokescreen for the club, which had lost patience with his reckless lifestyle and thieving.

"We held on to him a little bit longer than we might have done with any other lad because he was so talented. It was all a damn shame," says Nichol. "The thing is, he could have had a great lifestyle, everything he ever wanted, if he had waited a little bit and got on with his football."

Inevitably his parents have tried to make sense of his disordered life.

"I have beaten myself up enough times. I have finally come to the conclusion that nobody is trained to be a parent and if I failed, at least I failed trying," says his mother.

Trevor Ross disagrees that the divorce was the catalyst.

"It had nothing to do with it," he says. "He started stealing and everything four years afterwards. I can't see a reason why he used to do what he did; no one can answer that question."

He is baffled as to where his son's unsavoury traits came from. Psychologists said the stealing was an attempt to draw attention to himself. The money it provided also allowed Jason to buy popularity.

"He'd want the money so he could take everyone out. He thought it made him popular, made him the great 'I am'. He'd take 50 people out for a Chinese meal and pay for everyone. He needed people. He hated to be alone."

In fact, Jason was rarely alone. He was someone people wanted to be around. He crackled with energy. A night with Jason was a story waiting to be told. On one occasion he hired a suite at the most prestigious hotel in Manchester and drank champagne all weekend. He was met at the door by a chauffeur-driven limousine. He had bluffed his way through with stolen credit cards.

"They were going to catch me in the end anyway, weren't they?" he told his mother shortly before he served the first of two prison sentences.

One of his last girlfriends was 18-year-old Becky Crump.

"Jason was full of energy, always laughing and joking. He wore his heart on his sleeve," she says.

One afternoon while they were watching a football programme, Trevor Ross appeared on the screen.

"Afterwards he spoke about his mum and dad and told me all he'd been through. He said he'd wanted to be like his dad, to be a footballer, but that he knew he wouldn't be because of all his problems. I think he was angry that his dad had not been in touch down the years," said Becky.

Just before his death Jason had played for Bacup Borough of the North Western Trains League. His last game was an away defeat and on the return coach journey the squad was understandably downbeat. Jason learned that one of his team-mates played in a pop group.

"Jason told him he was a promoter and went under the name Tony Barcelona. He said he could get him a booking at the London Palladium. It did the trick and all the way back, the lads were in raptures," says Brent Peters, the Bacup manager.

A week after his death, Mrs Mizon attended a family wedding. They were a minute way from toasting the bride when they realised no one had ordered champagne.

"Your Jason said he knew a bloke who knew a bloke ..." she was told.

She raced to the nearest supermarket; still tidying up for Jason.

DEATH OF A LOCAL HERO

The Times, Saturday 9 March, 2002

Sunday morning, the world half asleep. An elderly man shuffles towards the newsagents in his slippers. He coughs and it sounds like a small jar of nails being rattled. Two men peer through the windows into the Poets Corner pub. They are early; it doesn't open until noon. Furious, one of them kicks out at a metal grille covering a supermarket window: Good morning, the Meadows.

The Meadows is a vast estate of pale brick houses and maisonettes close to Nottingham town centre. It routinely provides those terse two and three-word captions on newsagents' billboards: 'Gun Crime Soars', 'Drugs Den Bust', 'Man Critical'. There are good souls too amid the dissolution. A family makes its way towards the Bridgeway Hall Methodist Mission, the kids skipping ahead, their skin scrubbed and glowing like sunlight.

The Poets Corner is now open. Posters advertise Bingo on Thursdays and Karaoke on Saturdays. It is large and open-plan with bench seats against the walls and a mismatch of chairs jammed under tables. An old lady asks her male drinking partner for a Bacardi and lemonade. He comes back from the bar:

"I didn't want ice, you berk," she scolds.

The barmaid scoops them out. This time the lady calls him 'love' when he hands it over.

The pair of them open a newspaper together and study the horse racing form. She is extremely knowledgeable, quoting odds from long-gone races. Looking around, the room filling with smoke and bawdy bonhomie, she might like to proffer odds on someone famous, someone from a glamorous other-world, walking through the swing doors and making himself at home: 10,000 to one perhaps, a million to one?

Until a few months ago the Poets Corner and other pubs dotted around the estate had such a visitor on a regular basis. Pedro Richards was a member of the Notts County team that spent three seasons in the top flight of English football from 1981 to 1984. An assured defender, he played almost 500 games for County during a 12-year spell and is thought to be the first black player to captain an English professional club. After *Match of the Day* and a life less ordinary, he was back on home ground; unassuming, in and out of work but still King of the Meadows. Then he was gone, dead at 45.

Although he stopped playing just 15 years ago, Richards' story embodies the seismic cultural and economic shift in the professional game. A footballer can now sign a one-year deal with a Premiership club and be financially secure for the rest of his life. He will also have advisers and mentors and a posh car on a posh estate, miles away from places such as the Meadows. Richards had none of these, though whether he would have wanted them is another matter.

His was an enigmatic story and a personality to match. Even in death nothing was straightforward. He died the day before Christmas Eve last year after being injured three weeks earlier. The Poets Corner had hosted a wake for Shantelle Porter, a 17-year-old girl who had died after a road accident. At the end of a long day of drinking and reminiscing, Pedro slipped away alone. Soon afterwards he was found nearby clutching his chest. Rumour quickly wafted through the estate's maze of walkways and side streets: Pedro Richards had been attacked. The most outlandish version had him set upon by drug dealers and left badly beaten. Such was his status in the estate's folklore, his half-brother, Colin Ellery, had to quickly refute the gossip and would do so again a few weeks later, this time at his funeral.

"Names were being banded about and I was worried there might be reprisals and someone getting hurt. We heard so much stuff that was supposed to have happened to Pedro. I think the only thing we didn't hear was that aliens had picked him up," he said.

The police decided to investigate.

"We were hearing that he'd been beaten up," said Detective Inspector Tony Webster. "We couldn't find anyone who'd seen this happen and Pedro and his brother said the injuries had resulted from a fall. It's the sort of place where this kind of rumour is rife."

He confirmed that Pedro had never been involved in trouble with the police.

"I used to see him out and about in clubs when I was a young detective. He kept himself to himself and was a nice, approach-able bloke."

These days footballers rarely live in the town of the club they represent but Richards was resolutely fastened to the community that formed Notts County's support. The Meadows is yards from County's ground and for many years his family owned a shop selling washing machines literally across the road from Meadow Lane. As proof of his standing, when his teenage son's bike was stolen and word got round who it belonged to, it was found back in its original place within hours.

"Pedro was their hero," said his long-term partner, Lorna Kennedy. "He had a hell of a lot of respect from the local lads and they looked up to him. No one would hear a bad word said about him. They were all like brothers, one big family."

X-rays revealed that Pedro had two broken ribs. He was also taking antibiotics for a chest infection. The cough grew worse and he was admitted to hospital where doctors discovered a shadow the size of a 50p piece on his lungs. He had pneumonia. The disease took hold and within a few days he was critically ill.

"They called us in and I knew straight away from the doctor's face that he probably wasn't going to make it," said Colin. "They told us that only two or three people a year in the whole country got this type of pneumonia."

Pedro Richards died in his sleep. The grief among the football fraternity was deep and heartfelt. County supporters flooded websites with eulogies. He had been a loyal, talented clubman and had played the game sportingly. Most of all, he was adored because he was seen as 'one of them'. He lived among them, walked the same streets. He was the local boy made good, an irony since he was anything but local.

Until the age of 11, Pedro had lived in Laguardia, a walled town in the Basque region of Northern Spain. Set in the mountains of Cantabria, the area is famous for its Rioja wine. It is now a busy town but when Pedro was a boy it was the rural Spain of yore — donkeys used in farming; bulls let loose through the narrow passageways during fiesta time. He had been sent to Spain to live with his grandparents by his mother, Maria Pecina Torres. Maria had earlier left Spain to work as a domestic in England where she met Pedro's father, an Afro-Caribbean man with whom Pedro was to have minimal contact during his life. Spanish became Pedro's first language and, the same as his friends, he wanted to be a matador. He left the country at 11 to live with his mother who had now settled with Eddie Ellery, a Nottingham man.

Although he had seldom kicked a ball before, Pedro turned out to be a prodigiously talented footballer. He played for the top local youth side, Clifton All Whites, and was selected for Nottingham Boys. In both teams he played alongside Viv Anderson, later to win the European Cup with Nottingham Forest. Richards signed for Notts County and made his first-team debut within days of his 18th birthday. He was to remain there for the next 12 years.

"I first met Pedro when he was a kid on the ground staff," said Don Masson, his former captain. "I thought he had a tremendous future. He was skilful, fast, a good reader of the game but I don't think he ever fulfilled his potential."

Most who played alongside Richards or watched him felt the same. Soon after breaking into the professional ranks he found himself viewed — in the terms of the times — as a 'bit of a lad', a 'rebel'. Richards did not follow protocol. He spoke his mind. He was a footballer who didn't act or think like a footballer.

Already, the contradictory nature of his personality was evident. He was happy-go-lucky but sensitive, straight-ahead but complex. He didn't stop to think what was best for his career. He simply said it, or did it. Glad-handing and duplicity was an anathema to him. He grumbled soon after joining County, for example, that he'd been signed to provide succour to another black player, his good friend Tristan Benjamin. Later he declined an invitation to join an England get-together called by Don Revie; he felt there was a bias towards southern-based players. His views seemed unusually insular for a man of a cosmopolitan background.

"Pedro felt settled in the Meadows. He had offers from other clubs but he wasn't one for moving around. When he left Spain he was only a kid and didn't really have much say in the matter," said Lorna.

Away from the pitch he further challenged the stereotype. He claimed a love of gardening and was photographed in a match programme pruning roses. They were actually his step-dad's; this was the joke. He didn't drive, though if he had would probably have received a sponsored car. He bought an expensive semi-detached house in the relatively upmarket Wilford but after it had been decorated he declined to move in. He stayed on the estate.

"You've got to understand that Pedro wasn't at all materialistic. I don't think he was ever comfortable with that side of football," said Colin Ellery. "I remember being with him once when he was asked to sign an autograph. You could just tell he felt awkward about it."

In February 1985 Notts County granted Richards a testimonial match against Nottingham Forest. It was played at short notice and only 1,345 fans attended. Richards received £800, a paltry amount compared to the colossal sums testimonials now generate. He left County at 29 and drifted into semi-professional football and then out of the game completely.

He did not adapt easily to a life outside sport. He was out of work for long spells and reluctant to claim unemployment benefit. He worked intermittently on building sites but was considered down on his luck.

"The last time I saw him he was sitting alone in a rather seedy pub in the Meadows one Sunday lunchtime," said County fan Mick West. "He was very scruffily dressed in a tatty old sweater and sat there drinking on his own the entire time I was there, though he did occasionally speak to people he knew behind the bar."

Pedro's family says this was unlikely. They say he liked to dress casual but smart.

Although more than 400 people attended his funeral, including ex-players and staff, he was no longer in regular contact with many from the football world. Asked about Pedro, they all say how much they enjoyed his company, but then add that they had not seen him for years before his death.

"Pedro wasn't one to moan but I think, deep down, he might have been upset because he felt forgotten," said Colin.

Pedro's son, 14-year-old Antonio, is a member of County's School of Excellence. He has another son, Jordan, aged four, both from his relationship with Lorna Kennedy. If Antonio progresses to the first-team, the lifestyle and rewards are likely to be much different than those that came his father's way.

THE SADNESS OF CUP FINAL HERO

The Times, Monday 12 May, 2003

The ball was slipped through to Bobby Stokes. Alex Stepney, the Manchester United goalkeeper, expected him to either blast it or move towards goal with it at his feet. Stokes did neither. The match had sapped his energy and he could only stroke the ball forwards. Stepney, surprised, saw it roll past him and into the net.

It was the 83rd minute of the 1976 FA Cup Final and the game's solitary goal secured Southampton their one and only significant trophy. In the build-up to this year's final between his former club and Arsenal it will be shown repeatedly on television, written about in newspapers. Once more Stokes will be 25, slotting it home and skipping joyfully into the arms of his team-mates. He'll be shown in after-match repose, glass of champagne in hand, cigar in mouth. Footage of the homecoming will be dusted off when more than 175,000 fans teemed on to Southampton's streets, desperate for a glimpse of the kid with the cheeky grin.

Back then the Cup Final really meant something. England stopped dead still and a good deal of the world, too. It was the match of the year, the first day of summer; football and life wholly united. After the game, kids raced on to patches of grass, dads and grandads usually in tow. Wembley was on every street corner. There was always a commentary, delivered in a kind of dry shouted whisper:

"And McCalliog plays it to Stokes. He shoots — it's there!"

A year later there is another Cup Final, another hero. The same as birthdays, they seem to come around more quickly each year. Players such as Bobby Stokes slip from memory. Their names become answers to pub-quiz questions. While all footballers accept that fame is ephemeral, few have experienced the rate of Stokes' descent from glory. He made just eight full appearances for Southampton after the final and nine years later he was making sandwiches and washing up in an archetypal greasy spoon cafe. At the age of 43 he was to die in pitiful circumstances.

"It's a tough call but I don't think scoring that goal did him any favours," said Jim Steele, his former Southampton teammate. "There was nothing else in life that he could do to better it or even come anywhere near."

Although he couldn't drive, Stokes won a car for scoring the goal. It also won him free drinks for life from grateful Southampton fans. Unfortunately he took too many of them up on the offer. While his death certificate recorded bronchopneumonia as the cause of death, his friends agree heavy drinking was largely to blame. And a lack of will to live.

Peter Osgood was his best friend in the cup-winning team and they stayed close after retiring from the game. Osgood noticed the drinking had become excessive when he invited Stokes to help at his soccer schools for children.

"I caught him taking swigs first thing in the morning before the sessions started. You could smell it on his breath," he said. "We were driving in my car once and I had a couple of miniature whisky bottles in there. They'd been left over from a golf tournament. I stopped at a petrol station and when I got back they'd gone. I asked Bobby about them and he pointed to the can of pop he was drinking — he'd put them in there. He thought it was funny."

Until the last few months of his life Stokes was known for his gift of making others laugh. Osgood smiles when he recalls the time Stokes was the victim of a practical joke. On a team stopover he was served up a snack of dog food and beans. When he was told later, he claimed it had tasted fine; he was ill the next day.

"He was a smiley, happy person who was everyone's friend," said Mick Channon, another former team-mate. "He was probably too nice to be a professional footballer."

Channon and Stokes were apprentices at Southampton in the mid-1960s. Friends say Stokes remained in awe of Channon but his own career was not without merit. He was an outstanding schoolboy footballer, scoring 53 goals in one season for Hillside Junior School in Portsmouth. He played seven times for England Youth and was one of only two offered terms by Southampton after trials involving 600 boys.

His starting wage was £7 per week. He made his full debut at the age of 18, scoring two goals in a 5–2 home win against Burnley in April 1969. He went on to play more than 200 games for Southampton, forging a role as a tricky and industrious attacking midfield player.

A year after the final, he spent the summer playing for Washington Diplomats in the United States, before joining Portsmouth. It was an unlikely move considering their bitter rivalry with Southampton and he made just 23 full appearances. In 1978 he rejoined the Diplomats, teaming up once more with Jim Steele. Johan Cruyff was also a team-mate ("He spent most of the time sitting in a whirlpool smoking a cigar" — Steele) and he played several times against a New York Cosmos side featuring Pele.

Stokes returned to England and, as many ex-players did at the time, became a pub manager. The Manor House in Cosham, Portsmouth, is a typical estate pub — roomy, ersatz wood panelling, chips with everything. The sign outside has faded and slipped from its frame. Ask the current manageress if any of the locals remember Stokes running the pub and she'll tell you they don't. They do remember his cup final goal, though.

The long hours at the pub left Stokes and his wife, Janet, disaffected and they moved on after three years. While he looked for work, his cousin, Maria, asked if he'd like to help at her Harbour View cafe in Portsmouth. He stayed for nearly 10 years. The cafe is housed in a building shaped like an ocean liner in nautical blue and white. The 'view' close up is of backpackers leaving the Isle of Wight ferry terminal. Metal waste skips are pressed close to a wall, stained green from sea spray and rain. Farther out, the sea heaves to and fro and blocks of flats mark the other side of the harbour. At the cafe entrance is a banner: 'Under New Ownership'. These new owners keep a tidy shop, charging 70p for a cup of tea and £2.95 for a 'set breakfast'.

While he worked in the concrete boat, journalists often tracked Stokes down, usually at cup final time. He was obliging. He posed pouring tea, catching toast as it popped out of the toaster. He told them he worked from 7.15am to 4pm and mused:

"Once you wake up in the morning, swing your legs out of bed and stand up, life is what you make it."

He never asked for fees for his co-operation, which surprised his former team-mates.

"I was with him on the way to a presentation one time and asked him how much he was getting," said Steele. "He said he wasn't on anything. He was doing it because he was flattered to be asked. It was typical of his modesty."

Stokes began drinking heavily in the winter of 1994 when Janet, who had been with him nearly 20 years, moved out of their home in Cosham.

"Jan was the love of his life," said Stokes's friend, Denis Bundy. "She was lovely. Very bubbly and attractive but Bobby was a bit carpet slippers and a night at home."

Stokes fell into a depression that coincided with a series of benefit events in his honour — Southampton had prevaricated for years on this issue. He became extremely drunk at one dinner and had to be helped from the venue.

"It hurt him badly when Janet left," said Osgood. "They'd been together since they were teenagers. He wasn't able to cope on his own. He needed looking after."

Osgood was asked by Stokes's brother to visit when he fell seriously ill at his parents' house, where he had gone to live.

"I knew he was bad because he'd tried to play golf a few days before and had four attempts to hit the ball about a yard. He told me then that he'd been coughing up blood."

When Osgood saw him the next time he knew he was close to death.

"He was hallucinating. It was awful to see because he was such a lovely, lovely lad."

Janet Stokes (now Janet Hussey) had noticed a change in Stokes after his football career ended.

"When it finished part of Bobby finished. The only time the sparkle came back into his life was when he was back with the lads, doing charity work or playing golf," she said.

The couple hadn't had children which Stokes's friends feel may have contributed to his disillusionment.

"He was like a little boy lost at the end, thinking no one gave a shit about him. He'd given the club, with one kick, its most magical moment in history—this little lad from down the road," said Bundy.

When Stokes died the headline in the *Southampton Evening Echo* wrote itself: 'Death of a Legend'. He hadn't achieved repute like others—generals, doctors, politicians, poets— through great compassion, genius or determination. His was a sporting legend and they are more easily made, perhaps too easily.

* This piece took on a greater sadness when Peter Osgood died nearly three years later, in March 2006. I had met Peter in a pub near his home in Hampshire. He was good company. After the formal interview we spoke about his health; at the time I was researching a feature about the use of cortisone in football. He told me of the times he had been given injections before important matches, especially European ties. When he finished his career his knee had gradually seized up and he'd had great difficulty bending it.

As I drove away I watched him climb the short flight of steps back into the pub. He had to manoeuvre his leg carefully and I remember thinking that he looked much older than his years. Across the table earlier, eyes lit and a smile on his lips, he was his true 56 years but, watching him ascend the stairs, he could have been 20 years older.

FORGOTTEN MAN
STILL PICKING UP PIECES AFTER
TWO WORLDS COLLIDE

The Times, Saturday 6 November, 2004

The FA Cup Final, Saturday, May 18, 1991, 3.14pm. Two players collide, bang. They are Paul Gascoigne and Gary Charles. After a few seconds it is clear that England's most talented and volatile footballer is seriously injured. Left of centre, Gary Charles, the solid pro, dusts himself down, gets on with it.

The collision and the aftermath were flashed across television screens throughout the world. It quickly found iconic status, another in a series of freeze frames that would exemplify Gascoigne's career. We are as familiar with them as family photographs: Vinnie Jones grasping at his shorts while Gascoigne howls in pain; crying at the 1990 World Cup; playing an imaginary flute after scoring for Rangers; the 'dentist's chair' against Scotland.

The 'tackle' on Charles was a reckless, desperate lunge for the ball. In making it, Gascoigne tore a cruciate ligament in his right knee and many thought it might end his career, at the age of 23. In Italy, officials at Lazio, Gascoigne's club to-be, were worried. There and then, history was joining these two footballers at the hip, making a couple from two disparate personalities: Gascoigne and Charles, Gazza and Gaz, together forever.

Inevitably, the match between Tottenham Hotspur and Nottingham Forest became the *Gazza Final* even though his involvement had lasted barely 14 minutes. No matter, this was Gazza, to whom the word enigma was not nearly enigmatic enough. Then, and ever since, his cartoon life has flickered on, his heart on his sleeve, his troubles on the news pages, in books, celebrity magazines, on the television. Meanwhile, Gary Charles, almost out of sight, has also been colliding with life.

Charles left prison this week determined to put behind him a catalogue of undignified episodes. Like many former players, Charles's most difficult opponent has been time; what to do with it, how to fill slack days that were once tightly regimented. Since picking up a serious injury himself eight years ago he has, as other players have done before him, routinely turned to drink. In January he was sentenced to four months for dangerous driving and failing to provide a specimen. Eight hours after his arrest, he still had four times the legal driving limit of alcohol in his blood.

"I drank until I fell asleep," he says. "I'd been a footballer for all those years and it was all I'd known. I was trying to plug the gaps that football used to fill in my life."

His regular court appearances and two prison sentences have brought him the tag 'Boozy Soccer Bad Boy' from *The Sun* while his local paper, the *Derby Evening Telegraph*, has claimed that society is 'better off, and safer, with him behind bars'.

This scathing tone is perhaps understandable if you peruse Charles's press cuttings file. It proffers an unpleasant man, crashing into garden walls in his car, being abusive to police, arguing with judges who, when passing sentence, have referred to him as a 'lout' and 'a silly young man'. Reading them closely, it is also manifest that he has been given ample opportunities to redeem himself.

This profile doesn't fit the man I meet in a cafe in Derby four days after his release from Nottingham Prison. He is attentive, friendly, and likeable. He still has a sportsman's healthy aura, the eyes shining, the good looks intact. Unlike some footballers, he hasn't asked for payment or laid down conditions for the interview.

"I haven't actually hurt anyone," he says at several points. Except himself and his family, that is.

"I know I've let a lot of people down."

He began his career as a teenager at Nottingham Forest. Several clubs had previously turned him down because of his slight stature but Brian Clough, the then Forest manager, wasn't deterred. He told the press at the time:

"When he plays a one-two he goes like a gazelle. It's so effortless that at first it looks as if he's not moving, yet he's 40 yards up the field."

Days before the infamous cup final, Charles had been selected for the England squad. A friend had told him the news and it was confirmed when he bought a morning newspaper. On his way home from the newsagent's Charles was involved in a tragic accident. A motorcyclist clipped his car and crashed into a lamp-post. He died later in hospital.

"I had to go the inquest afterwards. It was obviously a really upsetting experience," he says.

He played twice for England under Graham Taylor before moving across the East Midlands to join Derby County and then on to Aston Villa. He picked up the injury that precipitated the end of his career while playing for Villa against West Ham United in April 1996. The ball was played over his head and, as he turned to give chase, his studs remained fast in the turf.

"I know it sounds daft but I looked down and thought for a second I'd put my boot on the wrong way round. I'd snapped the bones, the ligaments, the lot."

While he was on the ground he heard Paul McGrath, his team-mate, utter 'Oh Jesus' and some of the other players were so shocked they said it affected their performance. He did not play again for a year.

"That was hard to take. I'd been active every day and then I'm watching the other lads out there running about. It seemed to drag on and on. You ask any footballer and he'll tell you the worst thing is not playing, having nothing to do on a Saturday afternoon."

At this point he was 'drinking more than most' but still classed it as social drinking.

"I suppose I had the time on my hands and the money to spend."

He left Villa and signed for Benfica in January 1999 while Graeme Souness was manager. He was injured on the first day of training and left soon after Souness's departure, to join West Ham, the team he supported as a boy. Injuries continued to blight his career and in July 2002, at the age of 32, he announced his retirement.

"I went from having this fantastic full life to nothing, really," he says. "I'd be in dingy little pubs drinking on my own. I didn't even enjoy alcohol. I was drinking to forget."

He became estranged from his long-term partner, Michelle, and their three young sons. The drinking binges escalated after the death last year of his stepfather, who had raised him and his brother, Dean, from infancy with their mother, Rita. His biological father, a professional cricketer, had died of a heart attack at the age of 26.

Charles was imprisoned again in the summer for a breach of his curfew terms, removing an electronic tag to fly to Spain for a holiday.

"Prison is such a culture shock," he says. "It's just like you see in the films, walking around the yard and all that. When they shut the door at night it's a strange feeling knowing you're stuck there until it's opened again."

Now released, he is zealous about reclaiming his family and his life.

"I got the cones out in the back garden yesterday and was having a kickabout with the kids. It was brilliant. Then we were all digging, even the little one."

He also wants to spend time on a property business he set up a few years ago, buying and renovating houses. As he speaks, glad to be free and born again to sobriety, it is still difficult not to believe that it is much easier for him to fail than succeed and that those dreadful press cuttings form a sordid countdown. It is a paradox that prison for Charles was a similar environment to life at a football club. It runs by routine, the hierarchy is firmly established and the camaraderie robust. The next few weeks are vital. He has to learn to live without sport once and for all, to accept a life more ordinary.

* This article took months to pull together. I contacted prison staff, solicitors, friends and family of Charles's. When we finally spoke on the phone he was friendly enough but I was constantly given different phone numbers for him and he was often out when I called. Even on the day of the agreed interview I was unsure whether he would turn up. He told me soon after we began talking that he had been watching from outside the café, checking me out before deciding whether to go through with it or not. He was very likeable and candid and I had great difficulty seeing him as the offensive drunk portrayed in the papers. To think of him that way (and understanding it was part of him) was depressing; it made me acutely aware of the seductive power and destructive effect of alcohol.

Afterwards Charles accompanied me partway to where my car was parked. He was enthusiastic about returning to football. I told him I supported Rochdale and he mooted that he wouldn't mind playing for them. He asked who the manager was, how long it would take to get from Derby to Rochdale and was our current full back a good player. I briefly imagined him tearing down the wing on one of his typical overlapping runs. And then I thought: he's not going to sign for Rochdale, what am I thinking?

Regrettably Charles was involved in another drunken episode a year later. He denied assaulting Elizabeth Wedge, aged 43, in a taxi office in Clay Cross, Derbyshire. It was alleged that he punched and kicked her after she had teased him that he hadn't been good enough to play for Manchester United. He denied the offence, claiming he was an alcoholic and couldn't remember the incident. The jury at the first trial failed to reach a verdict but after a retrial in July 2006 lasting three days, he was found guilty. He was told by the judge it 'may be inevitable' that he faced a term in jail.

It was reported in 2008 that Charles had been attending coaching courses after spending time with Roy Keane (an ex-team-mate at Nottingham Forest) while he was managing Sunderland. Other reports had him running a restaurant in the Peak District and planning to write his autobiography.

IT'S BEEN EMOTIONAL – A TALENT
LOST IN TEARS, FEARS AND BEERS

The Times, Saturday 6 November, 2004

Football is briefly off the agenda but Paul Gascoigne, aka Gazza or G8, is still in demand, still in the news. He's doing as he pleases right now — the odd chat show, trips out with the family, picking the kids up from school.

His phone goes all the time; it probably always will. To get to Gascoigne you still have to go via his loyal mate, Jimmy Gardner. Mention Gary Charles to either of them and within minutes Gascoigne is calling you back. I tell him about the problems that have beset Charles in the past few years. For a few minutes, he can't believe it.

"This is all news to me," he says constantly.

This might be because within the game Charles was considered a quiet, reserved man, a stranger to trouble. Until a few years ago his press profile was negligible because as a young player he'd been advised by Brian Clough to keep his thoughts to himself and his team-mates. Dwight Yorke knew him this way when they played together at Aston Villa for four years.

"I don't think I could have met a better professional than Gary. At the time I was there he was exceptional on the field and a great lad," he says.

They last met up in London when Charles was with West Ham United.

"You hear through other players and read in the media what

happens," says Yorke. "It's terribly sad because here was someone who had the whole world at his feet but you never know what happens behind closed doors. There was never any sign of things going down a rocky road when I was at Villa and I knew him as well as anyone back then."

Gascoigne has said many times that the cup final tackle on Charles was nothing personal — anyone could have been on the receiving end. In fact, a few minutes earlier, he had almost removed one of Garry Parker's ribs with another lunging tackle. He admitted afterwards that he had been over-motivated, acting, in his own words, 'like a mad bastard'.

As he was being carried from the field at Wembley, Gascoigne asked about Charles's wellbeing. In his autobiography, *Gazza, My Story*, he wrote: 'At first I worried that I had hurt him, a young player just beginning his career, but he got up and seemed OK.'

The pair next met up a few years later when, by chance, they were on holiday in Florida with their families.

"I was laughing and joking with him and his missus, telling them he'd better not get too close to me, it'd just end up with someone getting hurt again. I was just having a bit of carry-on with them."

Charles has regularly been offered money from newspapers to talk about 'the tackle' but has declined for fear his words might be twisted to imply that he felt some resentment towards Gascoigne.

"This might sound weird but I've often felt sorry for Gazza," he says. "I haven't had half the stress he has. He can't do anything without people being on at him. Those that know him know what an honest bloke he is."

Gascoigne has had to deal with his own addictions and is not surprised that former players sometimes turn to drink.

"This is what happens with lads when their career ends and they've loved the game and lived for it," he says. "What are they going to do with the rest of their lives? Booze becomes a comfort. You have a drink on the Monday, another on the Tuesday and before you know it you're addicted."

He feels his most important move was to admit he was an alcoholic and believes Charles should do the same. I tell him that Charles did not refer to himself as an alcoholic once during the four hours we were together, and that he also believes he can 'sort himself out'. Gascoigne is instantly concerned. He asks me for his phone number.

"I've got to speak to him. I'd do anything for Charlesy or anyone in the situation he's in. You can't sort it out on your own."

He is on his way to a radio station as we speak, a 100 or so miles away from where Charles is living. He asks Gardner, who I assume is driving, whether they can take a detour.

"We can't make it today," says Gascoigne, disappointed. "Tell him to keep it together, man. I'm going to make sure I get over there."

---

* I'm not sure whether the pair did meet up, despite my giving them each other's numbers. Charles's mother called a few weeks after the article appeared and asked for Gascoigne's number which I passed on.

3

Close to the Edge

Halifax Town – Halifax Town (reprise) – Accrington Stanley
Barnsley – non-League football – Accrington Stanley (reprise)

★

TWILIGHT WORLD OF THE
CRAZY GANG'S COUSINS

The Times, Wednesday 9 April, 1997

The light is on but nobody seems to be at home. There are random signs of life, if they pass as such — two vehicles in the car park and a stack of empty milk crates by the main entrance — while, in the ground, a solitary figure in an anorak jabs the turf with a pitchfork. He points helpfully to a portable cabin at the side of the stand.

"You could try in there," he says.

This grey, nondescript structure is the last piece of England to remain forever Halifax Town. It is just a few yards from the pitch on which the club has played for the past 75 years. Touching distance almost, except touching is not allowed outside of a few hours every other Saturday. The pitch, the stands, the dressing rooms and everything within this natural amphitheatre belongs to the local council. Calderdale Council settled the club's debts of £375,000 in a straight swap for a lease of the football ground formerly known as The Shay. Halifax Town are strangers on home ground.

Halifax are, of course, not the only football club without a ground to call their own. Wimbledon, most famously, have managed extraordinarily well without a home and this is apt, for the clubs have a special kind of kinship. They are the football equivalent of twin towns. The link goes back almost two decades, to a time when they were equals.

On Saturday, August 20, 1977, the opening day of a new season, they met in the old fourth division. Wimbledon, after several valiant FA Cup runs, had replaced Workington in the league while, for Halifax, it was business as usual as they embarked upon their 47th League season. An open game ended 3–3 and by virtue of beginning with the letter 'H', Halifax were placed above Wimbledon in the table. They would never be so close again. While Wimbledon prepare to take on Chelsea in the FA Cup semi-final on Sunday, Halifax, who lost their League status in 1993, are battling against relegation from the Vauxhall Conference.

The chasm between the clubs cuts deep. Halifax have three full-time members of staff while Wimbledon have a squad recently valued at £50 million. Wimbledon's record signing is Ben Thatcher at £1.8 million while Halifax's is Ian Juryeff at £50,000. Wimbledon are going all out for the FA Cup and Europe. Halifax are all out for survival. What has happened to cause these former footmen of the fourth division to have such diametrical fortunes? The simplistic response would be finance: Wimbledon have had it, Halifax have not.

"That's not true," a Wimbledon spokesman says. "We might have a few bob now but we didn't for a long time."

The 'spokesman' asks not to be named ("Sam doesn't like us talking too much."). Sam, of course, is Sam Hammam, the Wimbledon managing director.

"In Sam we have got someone who was like Churchill in the war. He has his own little gurus who he consults but he makes decisions without going through lots of ruddy committees."

The choice of personnel at Wimbledon has always been inspired. From John Fashanu to Joe Kinnear, Vinnie Jones to Dave Bassett, the club has sought the charismatic.

"There's also a lot of continuity here. People stick around, especially behind the scenes. Sam has also believed in investing in players before anything else. We've always had a brilliant youth policy."

Continuity has not been Halifax Town's forte. They had 23 managers in the period between the Second World War and their demotion. Halifax did, however, have their own successful youth policy and for a long period this ensured bills were paid more or less on time. Pete Barrow covered their affairs for the *Halifax Evening Courier* during the twilight years of their League career. He believes the disintegration of their youth programme precipitated relegation.

"The juniors were a good team. Bill Ayre [the manager from 1986 to 1990] knew everyone at the club and made them feel like they belonged," he said.

Ayre's replacement, Jim McCalliog, concentrated on experienced professionals and this formula was further endorsed by his replacement, John McGrath, who disbanded the youth team. Many Halifax fans saw this as a near-mortal blow. In their final League season, with games running out, Halifax appointed their physiotherapist, Mick Rathbone, as team manager.

"It was an inspired choice," said Barrow. "The players loved him to bits and he brought a real backs-to-the-wall attitude."

Unfortunately Rathbone was perhaps too close to the players and some insiders felt he was reluctant to take the substantive action required. Town's final Football League game was against Hereford United on May 8, 1993. They needed to win but lost 1−0, the goal scored by a former Halifax player, Derek Hall. Wycombe Wanderers were promoted from the Conference and Halifax duly moved to semi-professional status.

"I suppose you could say Halifax have found their level in a way," said Barrow.

Barrow, a Barnsley supporter, is allowed this apostate view but to the fanatical this assumption of a 'rightful place' is an anathema. Dave Worthington, the commercial manager, is one of three generations of his family to have worn the blue and white of Halifax as a player.

"I just stood there devastated the day we went out," he said. "A lot of people were crying. We all went out for a few drinks afterwards, like you do in those situations."

The Shay, at least by name, is no more. When the council acquired the lease it became Calderdale Sports Stadium, though few refer to it as such. Derek Newiss, the club secretary and former chairman of the supporters' club, obliges with a guided tour. He has an extremely dry humour and a placid temperament; perhaps the ideal demeanour for a Halifax devotee. The offices have the scuffed wallpaper and cigarette-end shabbiness of a taxi rank. The directors' box ("Well, we call it that") is a collection of breezeblocks at the back of the stand. Foam is taped to supporting joists above the wooden seats to reduce the risk of a sore head. The decor throughout is a bizarre mixture of styles and ages — doors containing bubbly, frosted glass from the 1960s lead to dressing rooms with shiny wooden panelling, evoking the 1930s.

Optimism, the curse of the football fanatic, is alive amid the decay. The heart still beats. Plans have been drawn up for Halifax Blue Sox, Town's rugby league-playing neighbours, to move in. The youth structure is also back in place.

"I took this job thinking that we would get back in the League and I still think that," said Worthington. "Someone will come along eventually and invest in the club."

The link with Wimbledon continues, consolidated by the efforts of Robert Holmes, an estate agent with a shop in Wimbledon Village, who has supported Halifax Town for 35 years. He holds an annual fund-raising party and Joe Kinnear attended the most recent.

"Joe and the boys are always keen to support it," said Holmes. "They've never forgotten their roots and I think they genuinely hold a lot of affection for Halifax Town."

At some point this week Wimbledon's fax machine will shudder into life and proffer the usual good luck messages from Halifax Town.

"We always refer to ourselves as 'your northern supporters' club'," said Newiss.

The Wimbledon dream has come true and could once again embrace a visit to Wembley. The wait continues for Halifax.

* How times change. Wimbledon, of course, are no more after being superseded by MK Dons in 2004. A group of their supporters formed AFC Wimbledon and entered the Combined Counties League from where they embarked on four promotions in seven seasons to reach the Conference at the start of the 2009/10 season. Halifax rallied and just over a year later were back in the Football League ...

HALIFAX HAPPY WITH NEW
INTEREST RATE

The Times, Thursday 6 August, 1998

'It's Monday, be happy,' is scrawled on the notice board in the reception area at The Shay. No one at Halifax Town really needs the reminder because, at last, there is happiness in the hillsides. After a short spell in the semi-professional ranks of the Vauxhall Conference, Halifax are set to reclaim their place in the Football League.

As comebacks go it seemed about as likely as a return for the Raleigh Chopper or The Osmonds. Five years ago Halifax made a tearful exit from the Football League after 82 years of proud but inglorious struggle in the professional game. At 5.50pm on Saturday May 8, 1993, their supporters cried into the grass when a 1–0 defeat by Hereford United — combined with results elsewhere — condemned them to relegation. They slumped to the pitch, shaking their heads in disbelief. It looked like death. Amen to the Shaymen.

Derek Hall, a former Town player, scored the Hereford goal, via a scrappy, reluctant stab of the toe. Halifax supporters swear that they knew, just knew, that a former player would administer the last rites; it was more of their infamous bad luck. The Shay, they believe, is a place where hex marks the spot.

Even last season when Halifax strolled to promotion, there remained a sense of misgiving, a constant paranoia that a run of defeats was waiting to bring them back to their rightful place as professional losers. After all, success and Halifax Town went together like Emma Noble [model and socialite, briefly famous in the late 1990s] and a quiet night-in with a 1,000-piece jigsaw.

Suddenly and unexpectedly Halifax became a decent football team. George Mulhall, a shrewd Scot with decades of experience, was made manager. He saved them first from relegation to the Unibond League and last season orchestrated a no-fuss return to the League. They were unbeaten at home and lost only five times all season. The football was neat and sweet, the curse given a free transfer.

"It was very much a 'pinch me' type situation," said Dave Fletcher, who covers Town for the *Halifax Evening Courier*. "They got off to a good start, unbeaten in their first 15 games, and Geoff Horsfield was scoring goals from all over the place. The league was more or less wrapped up by Christmas."

Mulhall, typically, refused to countenance any premature celebrations.

"The fat lady hasn't sung yet," he told Fletcher repeatedly. As the wins piled up, the metaphor became more strained. "She's clearing her throat," he told a small press throng. "She's about to take the stage ... "

Finally, after a win at Kidderminster Harriers that clinched promotion, she sang the song of the Shaymen and even Mulhall was caught smiling on photographs.

"I do not bring fear to the players. I'm not one for throwing cups around," he said. "I'm strong with my views but I tell people in the right manner."

His secretary enters the room to inform him that a player he has been expecting has arrived. She's reluctant to utter his name, wary of a reporter's notebook.

"Och, you can say his name, this lad is deaf anyway," he says, pointing in my direction.

Among the papers on his desk is a lengthy list of players available for free transfer published by the Professional Footballers' Association. It is a non-Fantasy Football squad, a collection of journeymen and wanabees, jobbing footballers looking for a break.

"I phoned one lad. He wanted £55,000 just to sign," said Mulhall. "I told him I was wasting money on the phone bill just talking to him." His eyes light up again. "That was the price in June. I'm sure he'll be a wee bit cheaper now the season is upon us." When Mulhall played for Aberdeen in the 1960s he was paid £22 a week.

On the pitch Mulhall's strength of character was mirrored last season by Kieron O'Regan, his assistant, and two veteran warhorses. Peter Jackson held the defence together until Brian Kilcline, the former Coventry City defender with a pirate's haircut and smile, was summoned from his plumber's job as a replacement. Kilcline has now moved to Altrincham.

"He did a good job for us but I didn't think he had the legs for the Football League," said Mulhall.

There is another knock at the door. It is the ubiquitous, earnest not-so-young chap with an indeterminate role who can be found at most football clubs. He looks as if he has seen a murder out in the corridor. A badly washed kit is thrown down in front of Mulhall.

"Look at these, George," he implores.

A pair of shorts is handled suspiciously. It starts to feel like an episode of *Quincy*.

"It's just not good enough," Mulhall snaps. "Get on to them and tell them that we want a better job doing next time."

Halifax's sudden upturn in fortunes owes little to excessive spending and much to old-fashioned values such as team spirit and a good blend of players. Andy Thackeray, a veteran of 400

Football League games for various teams, signed when the Shay was at the first stage of redevelopment.

"It was literally a one-sided ground with mud heaps behind each goal. Once you got talking to George though, you got such a good feeling. He is a great fella and the spirit in the dressing room is really high," he said.

Since the merger with the town's rugby league club, Halifax Blue Sox, the Shay has been transformed and is now a compact, modern stadium flanked by the huge Halifax Building Society offices on one side and a steep hillside on the other. The players who formed the promotion squad have all re-signed, some of them leaving good jobs that they held down while playing football on a part-time basis.

Supporters are hopeful that Town will 'do a Macclesfield' and secure a successive promotion. Confidence is high but tinged by realism. Mulhall has a squad of 15 players and the switch to full-time will put a strain on resources. There is, however, a sense in the town that Halifax and failure are no longer synonymous.

"I was talking to some fans last week," said Thackeray. "And one told me that he'd seen a few kids playing on the park wearing Halifax Town shirts, and he'd never known that before."

---

* Halifax Town lasted four seasons on their return to the League. They finished at the foot of the table in 2001/02 and were relegated back to the Conference. In 2005/06 they made the Conference play-offs but lost 3–2 to Hereford United in the final. At the end of the 2007/08 season they went into administration after falling £2 milllion in debt. They were wound up and re-formed as FC Halifax Town, playing in the Northern Premier League Division One North. They were champions of their league in 2009/10, losing just two games all season.

ACCRINGTON STANLEY,
WHO ARE THEY?

The Times, Monday 18 November, 2002

It's raining. The nearby hills are lost to mist. Fallen leaves swirl in puddles. Could it be any more typical, any more Accrington Stanley?

"Do you want a Bovril?" asks Eric Whalley, the club chairman, self-made businessman and former manager. But Eric, it's still the cornflake hour, the day, at best, only half-awake. Bovril for breakfast? No thanks.

"I know but I forgot to bring the coffee," he explains.

This isn't quite what he says. Imagine the same sentence but dusted in swear words and you're getting close. Bloody close.

Everything in Whalley's office is painted job-lot white. There are no pictures, no family photographs on the desk. A television is unplugged and its screen pointed to the wall. The room is the man: unadorned, uncomplicated.

"The club are a big part of my life," he says. "My wife would say they *are* my life. I've been a player here, a manager twice. It isn't an ego trip, it's something in the blood."

The nation, possibly the world, feels the same way, for Accrington Stanley have never slipped from memory, despite 40 years in the sporting wilderness. Its name has become symbolic, two wondrously archaic words that set a rhythm of nostalgia, romance and northern stoicism. This season — by virtue of an unprecedented run of form — hope and renaissance may also form the story. Accrington Stanley are back, almost.

They are the leaders of the UniBond League premier division after only two defeats in 19 matches. If they maintain their position they will be promoted to the Nationwide Conference and come within touching distance of the Football League for the first time since they left the professional game on Tuesday, March 6, 1962.

Debts of more than £40,000 forced Stanley to resign from the League with 13 matches of the 1961/62 season left. An inaugural member of the Football League in 1888, Accrington had struggled heroically since their inception, caught between two better-supported East Lancashire clubs, Blackburn Rovers and Burnley.

Vincent Studholme, 75, is one of a handful of Stanley fans able to recall League football and the aftershock of its loss.

"I don't think I've ever got used to it," he says. "The town dies when it loses its football club."

In the midst of the crisis, Bob Lord, the then Burnley chairman, was invited to handle the club's affairs since it was assumed his connections with football's hierarchy would be invaluable. He recommended closure. At the time only £4,000 was required immediately and when news broke of Stanley's parlous state, offers of cash poured in. Alan Hardaker, the Football League secretary, refused to call an emergency meeting of fellow clubs. Instead he put the matter to the League Management Committee, of which Lord was an influential member. It upheld Stanley's resignation.

These shenanigans have not been forgotten in Accrington. Studholme is a quiet, unassuming man. He had a lung removed after falling through a roof and talks between wheezes and coughs. He has also had two hip replacement operations.

Mention Lord and Hardaker and he is suddenly fighting fit, driven by rage.

"Don't say those names in this house," he says. "I detest them. Bob Lord was supposed to be a saviour but he just wanted to rake off the gates."

An amateur team represented the town after 1962 until the club was reunited with its former name in the late 1960s and began a slow but steady rise through the leagues. Stanley moved to the Crown Ground in Livingstone Road in 1970, a former works pitch that has now been upgraded to a capacity of 5,057. Recent improvements have been funded by the £200,000 received from Southampton via a sell-on clause in the deal with Blackpool for Brett Ormerod, Stanley's former striker. Understandably, the club maintains a doggedly prudent outlook: only eight players are on contracts, none earning more than £300 per week. Several have Football League experience, including Mike Marsh, the former Liverpool, West Ham United, Coventry City and Galatasaray midfield player. John Coleman, the player-manager and a veteran of non-league football in the North West, has assembled the squad.

"We've been having that little bit of luck that all sides need and once we started winning it snowballed," he says. "It would be nice to reward the people that have stuck with the club through thick and thin."

While their heady league position is attracting attention, the chairman is fully aware it is the famous name that sets them apart. They became 'Stanley' originally because the club's founders were based in Stanley Road, Accrington, and there was also a pub in the area called the Stanley Arms. Whalley registered the name as a trademark when he took over seven years ago. It had come to prominence again in the late 1980s when it featured in a television advert for milk — a name check that netted Stanley £5,000.

Whalley isn't quite sure how to summarise the magic of 'Accrington Stanley'. On its merchandise the club volunteers, 'the biggest little football club in the world' and 'We Are They' — but neither seems completely apt. Maybe it is understood intuitively that it is something to do with pride and belief, that small things should be treasured.

BARNSLEY ON THE BRINK

The Times, Monday 3 February, 2003

The big question on Barnsley's official website this week is: 'Can England win the 2004 European Championship?' Fans are invited to key in either yes or no. As if they care. They have far graver concerns. The more pertinent question would be: 'Do you think this football club will still exist in a month's time?'

Barnsley are in a mess. It is less than five years since they were taking on Arsenal and Manchester United in the Premiership. They are now scavenging for points against the likes of Cheltenham Town to avoid relegation to the third division of the Nationwide League. Away from the pitch huge debts have forced them into administration and their story embraces every stereotype of football glory fading to ruin — rumours of double-dealing; a search for scapegoats; supporters' demonstrations; a mysterious overseas investor; hawkish property developers; and a new owner made as welcome as a pit closure. Even Toby Tyke, the mascot, scampered after claims that he was 'too energetic' in his distribution of sweets into the crowd.

Fans have differing opinions on the start of the fall of the Oakwell empire. Some trace it to Darren Barnard's penalty miss at Wembley in May 2000 when Barnsley were drawing 1–1 with Ipswich Town in the Nationwide League first division play-off final. Ipswich went on to win 4–1. Some believe that the sacking of Dave Bassett in December 2000 was the turning point while others go back to June 1998 when Danny Wilson defected to Sheffield Wednesday.

Wilson had steered Barnsley to the top flight for the first time in their 110-year history and, despite relegation from the Premiership, pledged himself to the club. He later claimed there was a special bond between Wednesday, one of his former clubs, and himself. The contract they offered, reportedly worth £1.5 million over three years, was incidental, he said.

His departure had a considerable effect on the town and club. Just months earlier the local council had planned to erect a statue in his honour. Now, 'Danny is Judas' was daubed on walls near Oakwell. The club and Wilson in particular had become a symbol of the regeneration of Barnsley. They had supplied hope and pride after the closure of the mining industry. After he left, five managers tried to stop the downward spiral as the club became enmeshed in football's great depression.

"Our mistake has been in chasing the dream to play in the Premier League," said John Dennis, the chairman.

Barnsley were not unusually profligate but found themselves in a volatile market created largely by the demise of ITV Digital. Paying £1 million for Mike Sheron in January 1999, for example, appeared reasonable but later, as the transfer fee system all but collapsed, he might have been available without a fee. The board sanctioned numerous transfers and the squad became an unwieldy mismatch of well-paid players, some earning up to £6,000 per week, on lengthy contracts negotiated before the financial crisis. Kevin Dixon is a typical case. He has yet to make a first-team appearance since joining from Leeds United two years ago.

"We call him God," said Alan Bloore, the chairman of the supporters' club. "Because we've more chance of seeing Him than we have Kevin Dixon."

Barnsley went into administration last October with debts of £3.5 million and a rolling loss of £200,000 per month. Matt Dunham of the administrators, RSM Robson Rhodes, didn't stand on sentiment, announcing:

"If there is no football the ground will be redeveloped, possibly as a supermarket or a retail park."

The players were asked to take a pay cut but refused, though they agreed a deferment.

"They have made commitments with regards to mortgages and other things," said Gordon Taylor, the chief executive of the Professional Footballers' Association (PFA).

Andy Marriott, the club's PFA representative, said their best contribution was to win games. Since his announcement they have won three times in 18 matches. The club's new owner said last week that the club was "paying Premier League wages and playing Sunday league football".

Various takeover bids were mooted but there was surprise when Peter Doyle, the town's mayor, was announced as the new owner. RSM Robson Rhodes said they accepted his offer because he could 'raise finance the fastest.' The Sterling Consortium loaned the money, investors who had lent money to Chesterfield and levied a high interest rate.

Doyle installed his son and daughter on to the new board while his grandchildren, Brendan and Caine, appeared with him at the press conference as he revealed details of his £2.85 million acquisition.

"I'm gambling with their future [his grandchildren]," he said. "We are going to be a people's club."

The people, initially at least, were unconvinced. Cynicism runs deep in Barnsley and the Doyles are well known in the town. Shaun Doyle, Peter's brother, is a former professional boxer and owner of a security firm that supplies door staff to pubs and clubs. Peter Doyle made his money in the gas pipe-laying industry, where a robust approach to business is essential. At one match, leaflets questioning Doyle's integrity were distributed. Doyle dubbed the agitators 'slime that crawls under bricks'.

Doyle's opening revelations led to more suspicion. He had split the club into two companies, one embracing the playing side (with its attendant liabilities) and the other for its assets, the 34 acres of land in and around Oakwell.

Fans thought they saw through his plan: he was going to wind up the club and sell the land for development. The profit margin, however, might not be as high as they imagined. While the figure of £20 million has been widely quoted, many think a realistic price would be half this figure. The buyer then has the additional expense of dismantling and removing the structure of the football ground.

Another unpopular move saw Doyle retain John Dennis as chairman who had been expected to fall on his sword. Dennis has been on the board for nearly 20 years and his father was chairman before him. Some believe he remains out of sentiment while others think he is desperate to leave the club in good health after the debacle of the last five years. He admits to being 'deeply uneasy with the situation'. For the moment he has Doyle's support.

"When you buy a hotel, you don't sack the manager, although I didn't know I was buying *Fawlty Towers*," said Doyle.

Shareholders are disgruntled because they have had scant information from the board.

"We got a three-line letter telling us we had gone into administration and that's it," said Benny Hill, a long-standing shareholder.

Many want to know why a reported cash offer of £5 million

from businessman Patrick Cryne was rejected several months before the club went into administration. Cryne, the chief executive of the club's main sponsor, iSOFT, has remained in the shadows throughout the affair and may still play a part.

The players, meanwhile, have continued to under-perform and have reflected the malaise running through the club. Goalkeeping coach Andy Rhodes resigned after fighting broke out at the annual Christmas party and team spirit has been hard to forge among players earning hugely disparate amounts of money. Glyn Hodges, the caretaker manager, is unable to sign new players because of a transfer embargo.

Doyle's latest announcement is that he is willing to bankroll the club until the end of the month but is open to offers and claims he has interest from an unnamed overseas investor with £10 million to spend. He appears to have won over fans with his passion and bluntness ('His management style is more stick than carrot', wrote one fan on the club's bulletin board) and has constantly said that he has the club's interests at heart.

* Patrick Cryne, as expected, stepped from the shadows and took over ownership of the club.

A LEAGUE OF OUR OWN

The Times Football Yearbook 2004—05

Solemn faces. Blokes in overcoats stare at their shoes. A few drops of rain come down. We're in Lancashire, England, Tuesday 6 March, 1962. Then the announcement: sad to say, it's over, finished. Thanks for your support. Please make your way home.

Vincent Studholme is now 76. He's never forgotten the day his beloved Accrington Stanley left the Football League.

"You can't describe it. It's an emptiness. I don't think I've ever got used to it. The town dies when it loses its football club."

We're with him, those of us that support lower league clubs. We're all big softies really, proper football fans, so when he talks like this, sitting in his favourite armchair, eyes a bit watery, we want to hug him, tell him we understand.

Accrington Stanley had acute problems that precipitated their darkest day. They were massively in debt. Thankfully the club survived and has moved slowly towards regaining its League berth. Still, whether through bankruptcy or relegation, the outcome is the same — an exit from the most prestigious sporting fraternity in the world. Worth crying about, then.

This season, my club, Rochdale, came perilously close to this very catastrophe (no other word will do). As the campaign drew to a close, defeat upon defeat, I had my first sleepless night caused wholly by football. We'd lost at home to fellow relegation strugglers, Macclesfield Town. We looked doomed. I'm not sure where the pain was centred but it bloody hurt. My insides were all mixed up, head aching, wanting to punch something, run somewhere, shout, cry, march up to Spotland and wail.

Until this point I'd dealt with our impending fate in two distinct ways. Firstly, I pretended the relegation places were already pre-booked. York City and Carlisle United were still below us, we had a squad too good to go down — the usual flannel. Then I embraced the new football orthodoxy. Hey, what's the big deal? The Conference is practically the fourth division of the Football League. No one can tell the two divisions apart any more. Come on lad, get a grip.

On that long night's journey into day none of this helped. Not one bit. Head like a tipped-over beehive, I realised how much it meant that my club belonged to this largely abstract entity, *the Football League*, the one and only. It also mattered deeply that we'd had continuous membership since we'd joined 83 years earlier. I know, you don't have to tell me: we've been rubbish a good deal of that time, never done much, but, come on, 83 years. Still there, still kicking.

Other Dale fans had already prepared for the worst. Football League clubs always bounce back from the Conference, they said — reinvigorated, tough as new boots. We'll be the Manchester United of the division, imagine that. Spotland, the non-League Wembley. No, no, I don't want this. I want every single one of my Rochdale programmes to have on the front, proud as punch, 'Nationwide League,' or whatever they choose to call it in the years to come. I want to relish all it confers on the club, the town and my support.

Poor Carlisle United, poor York City. They didn't quite catch us up at the end and were relegated; two clubs with long traditions and great fans. They don't deserve it. At least their places are being taken by ex-League clubs. So, welcome back Chester City and Shrewsbury Town, you've been missed.

Strange, how the top six sides in this season's Conference were all ex-League clubs. And that every club going down has come back up within a few seasons, quite often the first. Where is the evidence of this supposed parity between the divisions? When new clubs do enter the League they have the obligatory decent first season but thereafter do little to enrich it. Macclesfield Town and Boston United, two recent entrees, were the worst supported teams in the League this season and 12 of the 13 lowest League attendances were recorded at their grounds, along with fellow newcomers Kidderminster Harriers.

If all this sounds embittered, it's supposed to. I *am* bitter. Six pints, please. I can't do with the homilies about how 'nice' it is that the League receives new clubs, how it keeps everything fresh. This blather is uttered routinely by fans (usually passive, one-match-a-season wollahs) of Premiership clubs. Look pal, if someone was about to usurp your club, take your place, spoil your fun, you wouldn't be quite so chipper. You'd be at the barricades.

There is also the insinuation that because we're *only* Rochdale or York or Carlisle it doesn't matter quite so much. It's all a bit quaint down here at the other end of the League, isn't it? Not like supporting an Arsenal or a Manchester United where it really, really matters because it says so on the telly, the radio, in the papers, day after day. This is to overlook perhaps the most vital constituent of the League: that it does matter, all the way down, top to bottom. Passion remains outside the claim of wealth and status. It belongs to us all and England is unique in its depth of support. Nowhere else is a country criss-crossed by regional pockets of ardent, do-or-die loyalty to hometown clubs. The average attendance in the Third Division this season was 5,389. In Italy and Germany, clubs of comparative size can expect turn-outs of about 1,200 and 800 respectively. Not the same thing at all.

As someone with an undeniable vested interest in the machinery of the League's administration, I'm often teased, 'You hate non-league football don't you?' But I don't. I could cheerfully succumb to a Saturday afternoon watching Quorn take on Biddulph Victoria in the Trafford Factory Midland Alliance or Frimley Green against Chipstead in the (deep breath, please) Seagrave Haulage Combined Counties Premier League. Freshly-cut grass, stands the size of bus shelters, honest endeavour — all good fun. It's the other lot I can't abide, the interlopers-to-be, those buggers a bit too close to the top of the pyramid.

Bitter, for sure, but not peevish. Once they're with us, the Yeovils, the Kidderminsters etc, I don't draw a real distinction between them and the clubs they've replaced. They're in the Football League now, respect due. A game against them is as valid as any other. All the same, a victory over them is usually that little bit sweeter and leads to some playful chants implying they're not worthy of football's highest caste.

This might be what it's all about really: looking down on someone, feeling good about where you are and where you're not. Nothing shameful, here. It's the whole point, the very principle of sport. If you can't be the best you can be better than someone else. Ask Vincent.

NEW DAWN FOR FAMOUS NAME

The Times, Monday 31 July, 2006

The two Accrington pals are firing names at each other randomly, raking out memories: 'Mellor', 'Hargreaves', 'Watkinson', 'McCready', 'Mortimer'...

"Good players, they were," says Vincent Studholme, aged 80. Harry Stevenson, 69, puts down his paintbrush and reflects for a good while. All he adds, finally, is:

"Aye, they were."

The names won't mean much to anyone save for a small band of long-term Accrington supporters. To them, they mean the world. Harry and Vincent are at Stanley preparing for the new season, a season they never thought they'd see. Accrington Stanley are back in the Football League, 44 years after leaving it.

"I remember talking to Eric Whalley when he took over as chairman," Vincent says. "He said then he'd have us back in the League and I said, 'Give over'."

Vincent attended the fateful meeting at Accrington Library on March 6 1962 when the decision was made to resign from the League with the club in debt. He's not a man moved to overstatement but remembers it well:

"It felt like my world had come to an end, it really did. I'd been going up to Peel Park [Stanley's former ground] since I was nine years old. It was such a big part of my life."

He didn't go to another game elsewhere until the club was

re-formed in 1968. Two years later the new Stanley secured the use of a former works' pitch half a mile from their former ground. They are still based there today, although it now has the posh title of the Fraser Eagle Stadium.

"When we took it on it was a right mess," Harry says. "One day, and I'm not kidding, we dug up a whole railway sleeper from out there in the middle."

Not all of Accrington's residents were as respectful of the playing surface as the inaugural committee.

"I caught this lad going up and down it on his motor-bike one morning just a few hours before a match," Harry says. "I just stuck my arm out and knocked the bugger off. He said to me 'I'll get my dad on to you'. I said he could he bring up anyone he liked, I'm not having anyone mucking up that pitch."

The pair have no doubt who has been responsible for Stanley's return — Chairman Whalley, the delightful despot of East Lancashire.

"He doesn't have any messing, you know," explains Harry. "He has one lad tidying up the ground and I heard him the other day telling him he was taking too long to pull up the weeds. If he were here now he wouldn't have me talking to you like this, he'd be saying, 'Get that bloody painting done'."

Whalley's best move was to appoint non-league veteran John Coleman as manager in 1999. He has overseen their rise up the pyramid from the UniBond League.

"He's filled the team with Scousers," says Vincent. "I can't tell a word he's saying or what the players are shouting to each other but they've got the job done."

Do they feel the team is set fair once more for the Football League, beginning at Chester City on Saturday?

"To tell you the truth I'm frightened to death," Vincent says.

"We haven't got enough forwards. It doesn't matter how well you play if you're not scoring goals."

I suggest this might be Stanley's old inferiority complex, the feeling that they're not really capable of holding on to a League place.

"I know what you mean," Harry says. "What worries me is the support. They're a very fickle lot in Accrington. If we're doing okay they'll be 3,000 plus on here every week but if we're struggling, they won't turn out."

They both say they'll be thinking of Stanley fans now passed away when they take their seats for the first home match, against Darlington a week tomorrow.

"There's a photo of the original committee working on the ground and I think there's only two of us still alive," Harry says.

One of the men they'll remember is Dick Briggs, who, for a few years in the mid-1960s, waged an almost one-man campaign to resurrect Stanley.

"He was a funny looking bloke. He had a nose like a shuttle-cock and walked everywhere with his head down. He went from pub to pub in the town selling raffle tickets, trying to raise money to get Stanley going again," Harry says.

Dick died in 1982 on his first trip abroad, watching England in the World Cup. He was knocked down crossing the road.

"I used to tell him to get his bloody head up," sighs Harry.

This week, all heads are up in Accrington.

4

The Beautiful Game?

The literature of football hooliganism
Fathers, Sons and Football (book review) — the perils of cortisone use
racism — hooliganism in rugby league — football in Iraq (book review)
The Damned United (book review)

★

KICKING THE HABIT OF A
SATURDAY RUMBLE

The Times, Saturday 4 September, 1999

Bring on the bad guys. Better still, bring on the bad guys gone (allegedly) good. John McVicar, Dougie Brimson, repent and ye shall have wealth, fame and honey-tongued PR girls singing your song. More sugar in your tea, sir? More brutality in your books? Go on, be a devil. It sells.

Dougie Brimson, 40, former RAF engineer, married with three children, is an ex-football hooligan turned author. Readers gleefully visit football's dark side with him, simultaneously thrilled and repulsed, drawn to the gore like passers-by to a car crash. To open the pages of any of his six books is to flush an otherwise mundane life with danger, hostility, hatred. It's a regular One-Nil By Mouth, and Brimson is playing the Ray Winstone role; giving it some, having it large.

Hooliganism, like tuberculosis or smallpox, has never gone away but merely been displaced. There was an outbreak in Cardiff earlier this month, another in Lens last week. The national side is often the rallying call for the various 'crews'. England play Poland this week in a Euro 2000 match and it revives some mordant memories for Brimson. England's visit there in 1992 was, according to him, 'pure soccer warfare'.

"Luckily the lads stuck together when it mattered, from Middlesbrough to Millwall," he says. "When you go abroad it's like how much shit are you prepared to take? It's buried deep in everybody, every Englishman. You can look back at the Dunkirk spirit. How long does it go before you think, 'That's enough'?"

He is fiercely patriotic and believes England, his beloved England, is "treated like some dodgy aunt, chained up in the attic, never to be mentioned".

The football hooli-book is a literary phenomenon. More than 30 titles have been published since the genre was forged a decade ago. About 500,000 of these bleak and seedy titles have now been sold. Brimson is by far the most prolific 'writer' in the genre. He is football aggro's pornographer-in-chief, the quick thrill Mr Fix-it for the violence voyeur.

Most of his books have been written in conjunction with his brother, Eddy, five years his junior. They stare out from the back covers — heads shaved; inky eyes; brows knitted; we're-coming-to-get-you stares. If the picture doesn't do the trick, their publisher, Headline, has come up with a tagline of inordinate subtlety: 'Read this if you think you're hard enough.'

Within minutes of us meeting, Brimson has a mobile phone pressed to his ear. He's heard that football hooliganism is the topic on a radio phone-in and wants someone to record it for him.

"If you enjoy something, you always keep an eye on it," he proffers. "It is, if you like, the original danger sport because it is all about adrenalin and you never know what's going to happen."

He's a big bloke. Not particularly tall but Cinemascope wide; everywhere at once. His head is newly shaved. The accent is broken bottle North London. He drives me to a cafe close to Vicarage Road, the home of his beloved Watford FC. He stares wistfully from the window.

"I've run down this road many a time to get away from people," he says. "I've gone through that bleedin' graveyard over there enough times as well."

There are three subjects Brimson would rather not discuss: his sales figures, his earnings and his family. He has sold more than 100,000 books, which will have accrued the brothers at least £50,000. His family is not the gung-ho, latchkey amalgamation of hard-cases we might have expected. Indeed it provides a soft focus to Brimson that could seriously undermine his earning potential.

His father, Derek, is relatively well known on the English folk scene, touring pubs and clubs under the name of Derek Brimstone. Declare an interest in his services and he'll send a photograph of himself in a chunky sweater and denim waistcoat clutching a guitar. His PR bumph reveals: 'The entire show is linked together with tall stories, fast one-liners, tragic and comical tales.' Sounding familiar?

Eddy Brimson, a vegan, has now semi-retired from writing to concentrate on his dual career as a graphic designer and stand-up comedian. Another Brimson brother, Greg, is a respected sound engineer and formerly a personal manager to Terence

Trent D'Arby. There are five brothers and one sister. It all sounds a touch Bohemian.

"It depends on your definition of Bohemian," says Dougie. "We had a very enjoyable upbringing. It was chaotic at times but we had a laugh. I was used to coming home on leave and finding famous people sleeping on the settee."

Brimson joined the RAF at the age of 16 and served for 18 years. Visits home were spiced by forays into hooliganism, with which he draws a parallel to life in the services.

"I'd been in a regimented environment where basically you were told when to eat, think and shit. And although it's obviously not that strict, there are rules you adhere to and hooliganism has that framework."

He enjoyed the ritual — the chase, the implication of violence — rather than the real thing.

"I wasn't interested in violence for its own sake. It wasn't what it was about for me. The less violence I saw, certainly the less I was involved with, the happier I was. It was a kind of addiction, a Saturday movement. It was putting on a Pringle jumper and that was it until Saturday night."

In a football stadium or on a train station, gang warfare can appear random but it is highly choreographed.

"If it was just about beating up fans of other clubs it wouldn't be difficult to find out where they worked or lived and go round there and beat the shit out of them. That's not what it's about. It's about reputation. It's about humiliation. It's about bullying, because basically that's what it is."

While most hooliganism is fundamentally a noisy tribal stand-off, gang members are sometimes cut off from the tide and trapped behind enemy lines.

"There's a number of people who have been killed or stabbed or beaten up, or had the shit kicked out of them, and ended up maimed or whatever. There have been hundreds over the years," says Brimson.

His latest book, a novel, opens with an account of a brutal attack at an Underground station. 'Paul Jarvis' is kicked, stamped upon, and finally there is 'a crack as his head hits the hard concrete floor'.

Ian Marshall, a senior editor, is Brimson's mentor at Headline. He has no misgivings about sending him royalty cheques.

"I take him as I find him. His books are not about self-glorification. He is honest about his past, that he has done wrong, but you can't undo it, you can only try and make amends."

Brimson, inevitably, has now changed tack. No longer does he want war on the terraces or even in the all-seater stands that clubs were forced to build largely through the recklessness of his kind.

"I'm sick of going to places, coming out of grounds having to be quiet with my head down," he grumbles.

He has formed 'The Football Party', an anti-violence, pro-supporter pressure group. Gone soft then, Dougie?

"When I'm at home with the kids I'm as soft as shit, me." He almost smiles. The eyes soften. "I want to help stamp it out of football. I know the damage that is has caused to the game."

He lets slip about his next novel. I tell him it sounds suspiciously like a love story.

"I think it will surprise a few people, show another side of me," he says.

FAMILY AFFAIR REVEALS THAT
BEAUTIFUL GAME HAS UGLY SIDE

The Times, Monday 30 May, 2001

Book review:
Fathers, Sons and Football by Colin Shindler (Headline)

The scar is just about visible after all these years. It forms a small crescent in the centre of my right knee. I was 15 and through on goal. The defender made up ground and propelled himself into a tackle. We rolled over together as if stuck in an invisible barrel. As I extricated myself I noticed a stream of blood snaking down my knee. I was carried from the pitch, placed gingerly into my dad's car and driven to hospital to have my knee stitched up.

That clumsy tackle was the most fortuitous moment of my football 'career': it ended it. The doctor said I'd be back playing in a few weeks but I was carrying a far more serious injury — a fractured dream. A year or so before the collision, I'd sensed what football really was. I'd seen the dark.

Colin Shindler's new book, *Fathers, Sons and Football*, is that hard whack against soft skin revisited. Ostensibly it is a study of a dynasty of professional footballers, the Summerbees, but, more significantly, it is a head on a stick cleaved deep into the ground next to the swamp of the professional game. Beyond lies humiliation, mistreatment, insecurity and, finally, rejection.

Football sets men against men, on the field and off it. Professionals are locked into a world where your team-mate covets your place, where the spoken word is a half-truth or compromise and the next tackle could be your last. At pitch level it is a bear pit. At every turn in every game there is a decision that invokes bravery or cowardice, enterprise or caution. A footballer has to believe in an absolute right to the ball without fear of the damage he might cause himself or his opponent. He plays for the team but he also plays for himself.

Dulcie Summerbee, the wife of George, the full back, mother of Mike, the winger, and grandmother of Nicky, the midfield player, has endured a lifetime and a bellyful of football. To her it is 'a malignant, destructive force', not a beautiful game.

Of course, the financial rewards are now excessive and Nicky, unlike his grandfather, has been richly compensated for a life locked into the professional game. Last season, though, he was ostracised from Sunderland's first team and left to collect the training cones with the youth players after falling out of favour with Peter Reid, the manager. No sum of money can assuage the peculiarly crude humiliation that football routinely inflicts.

My 'career' ended before it started. My dad was the first to notice that the light had been switched off.

"You're beaten before you start," he'd say.

I argued back, but he was right. I was beaten when I saw our opponents; broad-shouldered, heads held back, eyes set straight ahead as if they meant business. I was beaten when they rubbed liniment on their legs and fastened on their shin guards. I was beaten when they ran hard for the ball, determined to win at any cost. I didn't *feel* like a footballer, never mind that I wasn't anywhere near good enough. A football pitch wasn't my rightful place. It isn't for most of us. The Summerbees belong there because they are hard and honest, belligerent and bloody-minded. Francis Lee said of his Manchester City team-mate, Mike:

"If you kicked him, he would definitely do you."

If a player does not hold to this maxim he is weeded out, put to one side. These rejects are good enough only for something distinctly secondary to football: real life.

Perversely, real life can seem a celebration after time spent in the company of the Summerbees — not just the players but their families too, for Shindler has assessed the impact the sport has had across the whole family. Admittedly Mike had it good and mentions 'wall to wall girls in miniskirts' and Nicky is a wealthy young man but the collateral damage is substantial.

Dulcie is now a great-grandmother to three-year-old Samuel. Already the family has noticed that he has unusually good balance when a football is about him.

"I hope to God he doesn't become a footballer. I hope I die first," she says.

No one is better qualified to speak on the subject.

THE NEEDLE MATCH

The Times, Saturday 9 August, 2003

Every footballer knows there is a price to pay. At worst the next collision could be the last. A whole career of tackles, twists and turns habitually adds up to an affliction described in the civilian after-life as 'dodgy'—usually a knee or ankle. Ex-professionals view these as industrial injuries. They rub at the soreness, free the locked joint and get on with it.

In recent years players of a certain age have begun to suffer debilitating medical conditions that they are less phlegmatic about. Fill a room with footballers from the 1970s and 1980s and they are noticeably different than most other middle-aged men. They look older. Some will limp or shift their weight awkwardly. Arthritic joints are nursed with elasticised band-ages. More than half of all ex-players contract arthritis before they are 40. In short, our former heroes are whacked out and they do not believe it is solely because of the wear and tear of their former occupation.

Their playing careers coincided with the introduction of a so-called 'wonder drug'—cortisone, a pain-suppressing steroid. An injection into the seat of a muscle-based injury had an almost miraculous effect. The player was soon off the treatment table, the stiffness and soreness gone, scampering around the pitch and scoring goals, winning matches.

"Before, you'd not be able to stretch or even run properly," said Jim Steele, the former Southampton and Scotland defender. "Afterwards you'd not feel a twinge."

Steele, at 53, still has the healthy radiance of a sportsman. He has arthritis in his wrist but otherwise he would appear to have been one of the lucky ones. Far from it. Steele has paid a debt to cortisone higher than most of his contemporaries. He believes it has made him sterile and this has been a significant factor in the breakdown of two marriages.

"Both of my ex-wives wanted children and it made it very difficult when we couldn't have any," he said.

His infertility was discovered in 1979 while he was playing in the United States.

"The specialist asked me if I'd ever taken drugs or been on hormones. I told him I hadn't, then remembered the cortisone injections I'd had. He said straight away that they'd caused it. He had no doubts."

Three years earlier Steele had suffered a serious groin strain that required a break from playing of at least six weeks to heal properly. At the time Southampton were embroiled in a relegation battle and could not afford to be without one of their most consistent players. Over the course of about six months the club doctor routinely gave him two doses of cortisone a week. The present recommended maximum dosage is no more than three or four injections per *year*. The procedure became so commonplace on Steele that the doctor sometimes answered the phone while the needle was still inserted in the groin, asking Steele to 'finish the job off'.

Afterwards, Steele would suffer acute discomfort — known as 'cortisone flare'— when the substance crystallised in his muscle. Once this subsided, usually a day later, he was free of pain and able to play. The soreness returned after the match, often of greater intensity because the injury had been aggravated while the pain was masked.

The effectiveness of cortisone meant its use became endemic in football. Gordon Taylor, PFA chief executive and a player from the same era, remembers it being, 'given out like cups of tea'.

It was an unpleasant treatment.

"The syringe was like something you'd use on a horse. It certainly brought tears to your eyes," said Taylor.

Cortisone was not designed to treat sports injuries. It became available in the 1950s to reduce inflammation around the joints of people suffering severe arthritis. It has no curative qualities but simply replicates the action of the adrenal glands, albeit on a massively exaggerated basis. Similar to many treatments it is the subject of debate within the medical profession but there is unanimous agreement that sustained use has serious side effects. An eight per cent reduction in bone mass was noted in cortisone users after four months and doctors report that bones and joint tissue on long-term users becomes 'like Swiss cheese'.

The PFA is well aware of the hundreds of players stricken by arthritis and other conditions possibly related to cortisone. Despite this pressing anecdotal evidence, Taylor is doubtful about securing legal redress.

"There is the question of who is to blame. Is it the clubs, the FA, the doctors, the drug companies or possibly the cortisone manufacturers? A long time has elapsed and medical records will be difficult to obtain."

Ex-footballers also have to prove that they are affected in greater numbers than other men of a similar age and that the cortisone is responsible, not the rigours of the sport. The enormous cost of a legal case and the uncertainty of the outcome make it unlikely that the PFA will pursue the matter through the courts. Instead, it is putting resources into warning today's footballers of the dangers of cortisone so they can make what is commonly known as 'an informed choice' on whether to consent to an injection.

Cortisone is still used in the game though it is seldom referred to by name. The chemical amalgam is much the same but the injections are now 'pain-relievers' or 'something to reduce the swelling'. Taylor believes regular testing of players and extensive medical check-ups will highlight cases of overuse.

Jim Steele is of a different generation. These safeguards were not in place when he played. There was no concept of informed choices; they trusted doctors and their clubs unequivocally. Most of all, they wanted to play and to win. He is disappointed:

"The PFA is absolutely loaded. You'd think they'd be able to do something about it."

He has formed an alliance with a group of ex-players but is reluctant to devote time to a concerted campaign. A year ago he took over the tenancy of a large pub in the Cotswolds and has settled down with a new partner. He is happy serving morning coffee to tourists and chatting with the locals in the evening, often about football. He doesn't want to dwell on the past too much or succumb to bitterness. He long ago accepted that he will not have children.

"There are enough rug rats in here to keep me going," he jokes, pointing to the slowly filling lounge.

BLACK PIONEERS DOWN AMONG
THE LOW LIFE

The Times, Monday 29 November, 2004

What did you do in the war, dad? A hell of a tour of duty, that's what: The Shay, Gresty Road, Prenton Park, Belle Vue — and I've still got the scars. Fourth Division football grounds in the 1970s were like those Armageddon science fiction films: all empty spaces, crumbling concrete and scowling misanthropists. As the fighting raged on the terraces, only the very stupid or the very passionate stuck with it. The rest baled out and it looked as if the bad guys in big boots had won the day.

Out there on the pitch it wasn't the time to be different, to stand out. Some players had no choice. Several years before Ron Atkinson and his much-celebrated 'Three Degrees' at West Bromwich Albion, black players had started to appear in the lower leagues. These weren't viewed in the same vain as curios similar to, say, Albert Johanneson at Leeds United or Clyde Best at West Ham United. These were largely British-born and here to stay. Many people didn't like it.

The abuse they received at Spotland, home of my club Rochdale, was repulsive. I recall Ces Podd of Bradford City defending a corner on the near post as people cascaded down to jeer and spit. The man closest to me was screaming, waving his fists. He smelled of beer and chip fat and slavered into my snorkel jacket. No one had the nerve to stop them because they were too great in number. The bigots held a comfortable lead over the decent.

On a few occasions in 1974, Rochdale had three black players in their team — thought to be the first time at an English club. These were largely spared abuse from home fans because, in the hierarchy of prejudice, club colour holds sovereignty over skin colour. The trio of Stan Horne, Leo Skeete and Tony Whelan were true pioneers, plying their trade within touching distance of hostile cranks in hick towns where the only black visitor year-on-year came wrapped in a football strip.

"I honestly didn't see it like that," said Tony Whelan. "It's only now looking back that you realise. I just wanted to play. It's true that in a game you lose yourself. You become so focused that you can shut most things out."

Come on Tony, how did you miss it? The Chicken George jibes from *Roots*. Your nickname of Urko, the war-mongering gorilla in *Planet of the Apes*. He'd forgotten about this. I show him a profile on himself from an old match programme that closes with the line:

'No monkey business on the field!'

"It looks bad now taken out of context but it was never vicious. It was a send-up. It really didn't bother me. If they wanted to have a laugh I'd go along with it. I know they respected me and that was all that mattered."

He prefers to remember that he was once the supporters' player of the year and cherishes a letter from a Lincoln City fan praising his ability. He recalls a game away to Rotherham United where he gave a witty answer to a local and every time he took a corner thereafter he was applauded by opposing fans. In the 1975/76 season he was chosen in the Professional Footballers' Association's divisional team.

"It comes down to whether you want to see the good in people or not. I've always tried to be positive in my life and it has brought me a lot."

Indeed it has. He is now deputy assistant director of Manchester United's academy. As a youngster himself he began his career at Old Trafford on the fringe of a first-team boasting Best, Law and Charlton. He moved to Manchester City and Rochdale and then played in the United States.

Whelan has watched racism return to the sporting agenda lately with wariness and is anxious that it remains in perspective.

"We fought all those stereotypes years ago — that black players didn't like the cold weather, that we weren't brave enough, that we could only play in certain positions. My wife was really shocked by the booing and monkey chants the black England lads received in Spain. She really felt sorry for them. It's weird, my daughter was looking at a team photo of me when I played at United and she said, 'Dad, you're the only black face on there.' I had to look again because I hadn't noticed at the time. You'd never get that now on a team photo."

* Racism in football was briefly on the agenda after several black England players were jeered earlier in the month (November, 2004) during a friendly match played at the Bernabeu Stadium in Madrid which England lost 1–0.

Tony Whelan was one of my heroes when I first started watching Rochdale. Although tall for a winger, he was extremely skilful. We talked for a good while and he made an interesting cultural point. He said he had served on many race-related football panels but his own experience was perhaps atypical of most current black players. He had been brought up in a largely white neighbourhood and there was a vast difference between his upbringing and that of black lads, mainly from London, who largely stayed within their own communities. It illustrated the complexities of the issue.

EVERY FAMILY HAS ITS
BLACK SHEEP

The Times, Saturday 25 June, 2005

Book review:
The Family Game: The Untold Story of Hooliganism in
Rugby League by Michael James (Parrs Wood Press)

The final whistle blows and we shuffle through rusty iron gates. It's the early 1980s and we are making our way from a lower-league football ground after another defeat. Actually, we aren't making our way. We are being marched along the pavement, all 20 of us visiting fans, by about the same number of police officers who bark at us randomly as if we are slacking en route to the next pile of rocks we have to break. As we veer slightly from the main group, a copper puts his hand roughly on my dad's shoulder.

"Where do you think you're going?"

I've never heard him spoken to like this before, even by my mum when she's in one of her worst moods. How will he react? He's a proud man.

"I'm going to my bloody car, get off me."

The hand is removed. The copper backs off.

Back then the nation didn't indulge in laboured socio-cultural deliberations on hoodies and their ilk. Stereotyping ruled. So if you were a football fan and attended matches, woe betides — you were a felon. There was no amnesty, even for sensibly dressed middle-aged men such as my dad.

Football grounds were furbished in the style of the local dog pound and police were encouraged to consider themselves extras in a re-make of *1984*. Clearly, you had to love your football to suffer this level of indignity and mistreatment on a regular basis. We loved our football.

Meanwhile, so legend has it, rugby league was a sport followed by men forged in the Corinthian spirit. Rival fans stood shoulder to shoulder dipping Wagon Wheels into each other's Bovril, cheering on both teams, happy clappy whatever the result.

A new book challenges this image. *The Family Game* by 'Michael James' is a familiar tale of ruck 'n' roll on the terraces, except this time the protagonist affixes himself to the divinity of rugby league. Scraps in pubs, town centres and outside grounds in the late 1970s and early 1980s are eagerly detailed by an author unwilling to lend his real name to his magnum opus. Perhaps this was a wise move because even before publication the partisans were mobilised, threatening in violent and abusive terms anyone — the author and the publishers chiefly — who dared to suggest there was anything violent and abusive about their beloved sport.

As someone brought up in a rugby league heartland, I see much to admire in its fellowship. Unfortunately it is often conjoined to sanctimony. 'There's never any trouble at t'rugby, not like football,' they say around here. As the author himself admits, hooliganism in rugby league is small-scale. All the same, it exists and this serves to highlight the hypocrisy of its crowing over football. The sport may be less moneyed and intrinsically more mud and thud than our national game but its players and supporters are that same rough mix of men and women involved in any sport: greedy, generous, flawed, selfish, goodnatured, crude, loyal, capricious. And, like it or not, some of their number will be prone to violence.

FORCES OF CHAOS

The Times, Saturday 30 July 2005

Book reviews:
Baghdad FC, Iraq's Football Story
by Simon Freeman (John Murray)
Pointless, a Season with Britain's Worst Football Team
by Jeff Connor (Headline)

Sport is burdened with expectations. It is presumed to excite, unite, heal and provide redemption. When it fails, as it has in Iraq, it is a catastrophe. If people cannot come together to play or watch others play, hope has lost its best ally.

Iraq is a football-loving nation. In 2002 the national team was ranked 51st in the world, higher than both Scotland and Wales. Before the war, crowds of up to 50,000 flocked to support clubs that had evolved from institutions such as universities, police and the army. Last October the national league was reconvened, though sensibly divided into four regional divisions. Almost inevitably it foundered. Teams struggled to negotiate road-blocks and potholes to reach grounds; matches were abandoned partway through; attendances (understandably) were low if not non-existent; and one club, Diwaniya, disappeared altogether.

The problem is more complex than sheer logistics and security fears. If sport is a barometer of a country's health, all that is wrong about Iraq is wrong with its football. The corruption and paranoia engendered under the regime of Saddam Hussein remains, though perhaps in a more invidious guise.

Saddam's sadistic son, Uday, used sport as his plaything. His megalomania had no limits. He took over a club, al-Karkh, changed its name and forced the country's best players to join. Matches were fixed and he incarcerated under-performing players: two days for a defensive mistake, three weeks for a missed penalty. Players were sometimes ordered to attend 'training sessions' in the early hours when Uday would join in. No player dared tackle him and risk a beating with lengths of cable or being forced to kick a concrete 'football'.

The game's administration was choked with Baath Party members, levering money and prestige from their association with Iraq's feted sportsmen. Genuine football men, such as Ammo Baba ('the Arab Pele'), had a choice: yield and appear complicit in the gangsterism or abandon the sport. Protest was not an option; dissenters were routinely executed. Baba, who had coached the national side on seven occasions, escaped physical punishment but under Uday's tyranny his dignity was undermined until he succumbed, like many others, to self-delusion and paranoia.

The Coalition Provisional Authority (CPA) recognises that the resumption of regular football is a vital step towards 'normalising' Iraq. Like much of the coalition's strategy, the handshake has sometimes been a punch. At first they used the people's national stadium, the al-Shaab, as a parking lot for tanks, causing extensive damage which has taken months to repair. Although American soldiers have thrown footballs to children by the roadside as gifts, many Iraqis feel their invaders' historic indifference to football is further evidence of a cultural chasm.

A Scottish solicitor on secondment to Iraq, Mark Clark, is

trying valiantly to connect the various factions within the Iraqi Football Association (IFA). He is, like those supervising the police and other state institutions, finding it a dispiriting task. A collection of individuals, from shysters to dreamers, has moved into the vacuum, eager to lead Iraqi football (which is hugely popular across many countries when televised) from collapse into the arms of corporate endorsement. A typically bungled episode saw Iraq arrive in England last summer for a 'Goodwill Tour'. It closed ignominiously with a match played against part-time players in front of 2,500 people (all allowed in free) at Macclesfield Town. Amazingly, the team boarded the plane in Iraq without a doctor and interpreter so their spaces could be taken by various IFA hangers-on who left England without paying a string of bills.

The years of neo-fascism have left a legacy of fear, partisanship and suspicion deep within the psyche of Iraq's people. The chosen few who 'did well' under the old regime are reluctant to see power wrested away while the majority are unwilling to forgive, riven by mistrust and cynicism. Simon Freeman, after 200-odd pages of intelligent and thorough research, can conclude only that in football, the same as everything else in Iraq, the situation is 'mad, and sad'. For now, there is no more to say.

If the word 'hopeless' comes in its absolute, most sorrowful definition when applied to Iraq, it takes on a bracing, comic air affixed to East Stirlingshire FC. They are, officially and conclusively, *hopeless*. They pay their players £10 a week, house their directors in a shack and closed their season at the bottom of Scotland's third division with a goal difference of minus 56.

Jeff Connor shamelessly bunged the club £2,000 for the penance of spending a season with them. He found precisely what you might expect at football's fag end: the mad, the sad, the dangerous and the dodgy. The 'characters' step forward obligingly. Dennis Newall, the manager, is the master of profanities while Alan Mackin is that serpent among football folk, the property developer-turned-club chairman. The supporting cast is direct from the latest Mike Leigh film, passionate but slightly dotty in their six-toggle, knee-length, sand-coloured duffel coats. And that's just the players.

Connor, as he is duty-bound, plays it for laughs. The chubby striker is told to 'pretend the ball's a pie' and when the goalie is injured the sympathetic cry is, 'Call the vet'. Conversely, the tour of Scotland's dingy footballing outposts and the tough towns they represent is baleful. At least the games are completed, however, and everyone gets home safely. They dream of such things in Baghdad.

THIS UPSPORTING LIFE

The Times, Saturday 9 September, 2006

Book review:
The Damned Utd by David Peace (Faber and Faber)

Football books are habitually the bastions of orthodoxy: play it tight, keep it solid at the back and let's hope for a sneaky win. Enter David Peace and a bloody-minded resolve to eschew the metaphorical 4−4−2.

Appropriately, he has brought to the genre the maverick properties of his protagonist, Brian Clough. The outcome is an expansive and ambitious piece of work dropping between fact and fiction, biography and novel, where two time frames run in parallel, perspectives alternate and no shirking at the back, young man.

In itchy, microscopic detail Peace focuses on Clough's 44 days as manager of Leeds United in the late summer of 1974. It was a disastrous union, for Clough reviled all that Leeds epitomised: their flintiness, their conceit, their dishonesty. Famously, he told them to throw away medals won under their former manager, his nemesis Don Revie, because they had been secured by 'bloody cheating'. Clough was going to make 'dirty Leeds' beautiful, at whatever cost.

Peace has researched his subject assiduously, listing 36 source books at the back of his own, among them David Storey's *This*

Sporting Life and John Braine's *Room at the Top*. He has borrowed their arid expressiveness and sense of place and set it to a rhythm of repetition similar to WH Auden or Tony Harrison. The prose is like studs clank-clanking on a changing room floor, always alliterative. Mostly this rich fusion is satisfying but — similar to any work with a bold stylistic objective — it grates sporadically and the exercise can eclipse the story.

The wide-screen imagination is all his own of course and he lays it out unfettered. His ability to 'become Clough' is disconcertingly convincing and this characterisation forms the book's dynamism. The only hitch of presenting such a well-drawn portrait, especially for the sport-informed reader, is extricating the real Clough from the 'fictional' one. While marvelling at Peace's inventiveness and recognising the sanctity of artistic licence, the reader is often nagged by the thought (and consequently drawn away from the narrative): is this real or made up?

At least Peace's approach sidesteps the converse problem of most works of sports fiction where setting it in an imaginary world lends it an unshakeable comic value. However realistic and liniment-soaked the text, as soon as an author mentions a game against Ironcastle United or an away trip to Cromford Bridge, believability ebbs away.

Since Clough is no longer with us and therefore outside the dominion of libel law, Peace is at liberty to portray him as he wishes, which is generally unfavourably. We are all familiar with his outsize ego but the alcoholism, greed, selfishness and stupidity is also finely detailed; maybe it's in those other 34 books and Peace has merely condensed the blemishes into a bruise. Only in his dealings with his family, especially his sons, are we shown Clough's considerate side. In the midst of the rants and rows and smashed up office furniture, he invariably has a pat on the head, a ruffle of the hair, for an offspring.

Faber, the publisher, has presumably had its lawyers rake through the text for potential defamation of those still alive. Johnny Giles, for example, is related as sly and manipulative and few players or managers have dignity or decency painted upon them. They are almost all universally hard, out for themselves, fiddling, conniving and getting their retaliation in first.

Peace understands implicitly that football clubs are mini Roman empires with shin pads instead of shields, tracksuits instead of togas. Clough, therefore, is the emperor back from conquering foreign territories, bestowed a kingdom where he is despised by his subjects. In the shadows lurk usurpers such as Giles, Bremner, Lorimer; men with a glint in their eye, a knife in their hands. Clough deserves his downfall (albeit with a hearty pay-off) because, the same as many visited by greatness, he fails to recognise its limits, to understand where confidence runs into arrogance and that expediency is superior to bravado.

Each year, one or two football books cross over to mainstream appeal and Peace's is well positioned to make this journey. He has found himself one of sport's most intriguing stories, teeming with characters and sub-plots, and set about it with panache. True football lovers will feel that in his scramble to stack high bricks fired in bleakness, he has neglected the joy of the game, the humour, but that is for another book, another story. This one knows that its place is with the avaricious and the megalomaniacs, sifting briskly through the grime and happy to be there.

5

The Business of Football

*The press pack — the commercialisation of football — Scorcher, RIP
the Football Museum — boys' football — Best and Edwards
(book review) — subbuteo — Bob Mountford*

★

RUNNING WITH THE PACK

FourFourTwo, January 2000

Poor sod, he didn't stand a chance. I was on his back in a second, grabbing at his clothing. Instinctively, he turned around, fists clenched, bewildered, out for revenge.

"Sorry mate, I lost my footing," I pleaded. His face was on fire, his features bent out of shape.

"Just be bloody careful next time."

The press box at Sunderland's old ground, Roker Park, was notoriously cramped. Once in situ, you stayed put. It was a bit like one of those old prison movies — attempts to escape were futile. If you needed to take a leak, an empty crisp bag was the only option.

Foolishly I had chosen to walk the 'plank' — a thin strip of wood placed inches away from a line of reporters on which they had plonked their notebooks and Prozac. Falling on the bloke from *The Telegraph* was the only way I could save myself from possibly breaking a few ribs. No choice at all, really. Afterwards, nothing was said. Accidents happen. Especially when you're part of the press pack, specifically the rock-hard, up-for-it, no-nonsense football sub-sect.

I spent two years running with the pack (well, kind of limping along at a comfortable distance) for *The Times*, covering the northern patch, a geographical area stretching from Filbert Street to St James's Park. Oh, the laughs, the japes, the scrapes. Except it wasn't like that. It was actually quite a slog, and often pretty disheartening.

At one of my first games I inadvertently positioned myself between two top buddies in the press box. They didn't let my presence spoil their game plan. They spoke across me, discussing last night's curry in great detail. I didn't exist. This was my welcome, or, more accurately, unwelcome to the pack, a world where the new boy is a nobody until its hierarchy deem otherwise.

Initiation takes years. They have to believe that you are trustworthy (you won't sneak Alan Shearer into a side room for a quick exclusive); deferential ('Bob from the *Mail* sits there, he'll want a word with you if you take his seat'); and, finally, that you aspire to caricature. They expect a certain force of personality, that you are so keen to join their rank you will become bullish, cranky, loud, a cartoon with a notebook.

Individually, most football writers are decent enough. They have been bullied into flinty camaraderie by circumstance. Much like the sport itself, it is a highly pressured occupation. Deadlines are tight, fuses short. Imagine: big European tie, Sports desk suddenly demand an extra 300 words. The match goes into extra-time, then penalties. Five minutes before deadline, your laptop crashes. Some prat has got his leg trapped around your phone lead and wrenched it out of the socket. You're screaming every swear word you've ever heard into his face, which is inches away. Then Sports desk phone again and they are screaming too, blue bloody murder. At this point, you're dead anyway. More or less. When you read your report the next day, it will feel as if someone else wrote it. Someone else did, a stress junky in an overcoat with a bad temper.

Most football writers are under contract to individual newspapers but many are freelance and are paid on a match-by-match basis. The fee from national papers varies from £60 to £150 for a report, depending on length. Hmmm, not bad for 90 minutes work. But this is to overlook the travelling. It can often take most of a day to travel to and from a ground. There are other peripheral hassles: the traffic jam on the motorway; the rat-scurry to find a parking space; the missing press ticket at reception; someone in your seat in the press box; your phone going wonky. Arrggh.

In practice, reporters don't see much of the game they are covering. They spend most of the time writing and, out of necessity, it is broken down into a series of incidents that will make neat, punchy paragraphs. Very rarely is there any kind of aesthetic pleasure. Additionally, reporters are denied the privilege of partisanship. It can be a torment to cover a game — no matter how supposedly glamorous the location — when your own team is slogging it out somewhere else. Many times, for instance, I have been at Anfield or Old Trafford and dreamed forlornly of being with my beloved Rochdale at Gigg Lane, the Moss Rose or wherever.

Within the pack there are several cliques. The lowest caste is made up of reporters from local papers. They are plundered for their local knowledge but later elbowed out of the way if they fall between a national hack and a player giving an impromptu interview. The tabloid writers are, typically, the most inveterate and gung-ho. Like footballers, they have nicknames and live fast. They are quick-witted and sharp, usually filing reports while a match is in progress. This requires a great deal of skill and clarity of thought. They have scant regard for their broadsheet peers who are largely viewed as effete. A common dig is that broadsheet reports are too ornate, with precious attention to the mechanics of a match. All those adjectives and descriptions of the scones in the pressroom — backs to the wall, lads!

Between games, full-time football writers are expected to file stories on a daily basis. The country is divided up and a reporter 'adopts' a handful of clubs on his patch. There are several essential sources of information they all use — Clubcall, web sites, fanzines and local newspapers. Outside these they develop a network of contacts based in and around clubs. They form quasi-friendships with club employees, sometimes paying 'tip' fees for snippets of information or a player's home number. Contacts are protected and there is a fierce code of honour among this training ground cabal. It might seem unlikely but few reporters would file a story that did not contain at least a tenuous relationship with the truth. Again, it may surprise many but papers are concerned about their credibility and too many unsubstantiated stories with the by-line 'W. Mitty' ultimately affect sales.

Players are generally reporter-friendly despite their supposed antipathy. Most will stop for a chat after training or a match and don't insist on contracts or payment; in fact, they seldom ask which paper you are with. A lengthy, exclusive interview is a different matter and will usually incur either a fee or a plug for a corporate sponsor. Much is done on trust and it is rarely breached. Most of the controversial stories about footballers emanate from sources outside the game and football writers openly criticise their news-hound counterparts. They quite like their cosy, insular, all-pals-together boot room world. After-match press conferences, for example, are routinely benign. More time is spent on a run-through of the injury list than the incident in the communal bath involving three blondes and a Swedish TV camera crew.

Often, there is collusion between players (or their agents) and reporters. They will hint that a player is unsettled to alert other clubs of his availability — this might galvanise a transfer or improve an agent's negotiating power. Reporters, since they can become confidantes of players and managers, sometimes become unlikely go-betweens, piecing together transfers.

Print journalism was once a major constituent of football, indeed part of its fabric. Its role has been greatly reduced by a deluge of information outlets, among them television, radio, Teletext and the Internet. Press facilities still exist at grounds but this is a historical debt rather than a real endorsement. Football clubs are obsessed with control and many are frustrated that press publicity does not garner them any direct revenue. Nor do they hold any sway over the portrayal of their club in print. Before too long, a rugged financier will surely demand that newspapers pay for their press season tickets. The year after, he'll shut the press box down, put glass in front of it and double his money by selling it off as a hospitality suite. Press? Who needs it? Troublesome gits.

Until that ghastly day, clubs should emulate the hospitality of Leeds United. At half-time there is a hurried exodus as the press corps scurries down to tuck into steaming hot pots. Chips, peas and tureens; no wonder their upturn in form has been so widely exalted. We love Leeds. They also had the foresight to enclose their press box and provide tip-up cinema seats.

Everyone stays warm and dry and happy: Leeds, Leeds, Leeds!

The friendliest doorman is the cheerful chap at Old Trafford. Sure, we all know the club is generally a PR trouser accident, but this is a genuinely kind soul. He smiles as he checks your press pass and gladly hands over your free programme. At other clubs, they are left in boxes and often dished out grumpily. The choice of grub is peculiar at United — the odd Bakewell tart, a flaky sausage roll — the kind of fare rustled up on a quick dash around Spar. Strange catering for a global institution. Quite endearing too.

Roker Park, of course, is no more, but press boxes designed by sadistic architects are still with us, even at newly built stadia. Middlesbrough's Riverside is another bizarre experiment in people and space. Basically, not much space, lots of people, watch them fall over one another. The box at Bolton's Reebok is so high that reporters are pre-warned about nosebleeds and handed nets to catch pigeons. Port Vale's press 'facilities' are legendary. Two portable sheds are perched on the main stand. When the wind blows nervous glances are exchanged and someone is dispatched to check that the ladder down is still in place. Ooh, the glamour.

The football hack's vocabulary in full:

Cross-fertilisation: a rather grand term for pilfering a story from one paper and flogging it somewhere else.

Down-page: unimportant story given little emphasis: e.g. 'Fifa Fiddles Millions.'

Exclusive: a few hacks band together and decide whose turn it is to show off to Sports desk by going live first with a story.

Flagged up: when a story is given a brief plug on the front page.

Lead: main story on the page. E.g. 'Beckham Buys Bread From Shop Shock.'

Line: the thrust of a story.

Pay-off: closing paragraph. A good one might be: 'And he later regained his sight'. A bad one: 'It was Leicester's second consecutive win by two clear goals this season.'

Runner: a report filed at regular intervals during a match. Not good for the blood pressure and best undertaken with a nurse on hand.

Spike/kill: when a story is dropped abruptly. One minute it's wanted sooner than now but just as you're set to deliver: "Oh, we'll save it for a quiet day." This quiet day is an ethereal, nay, mythical thing, man.

Sports desk: misanthropists in carpet slippers and bathrobes sitting in air-conditioned offices. Think of those all-powerful, out-there gods in *Jason and the Argonauts* meddling with people's destinies. You've got it.

Stats: who are we to judge, especially when a player's marks often have to be phoned over up to 30 minutes before a game finishes? Scored a hat-trick in the last five minutes, mate? Tough, six out of 10 it is!

Top: the opening few paragraphs.

Topspin: the degree to which a story is twisted, slanted and generally buggered about with to make it, as they say — sexy.

FOOTBALL MATCH MADE IN
FINANCIAL HEAVEN

The Times, Tuesday 16 May, 2000

The world is football-shaped. Where there was once a game, there is now a phenomenon. In your face and in your pocket: eat it, drink it, buy it, then auction off the television rights.

A regular gold rush assortment of conglomerates, strategists, prospectors, fast-hands and hangers-on has formed in the vanguard of this upsurge in popularity and profitability. The players, poor souls, are caught in possession (of a great deal of money), surrounded by a swarm of agents, advisers, accountants, press officers, solicitors, sponsors, car dealers and estate agents. Kicking a football must be a beautiful release.

Historically, players have been coy about their earnings, muttering about the shortness of their career or the sport's inherent physical dangers. No longer do they try to excuse their wealth.

"The money is obscene now. You never used to mind in years gone by when top players were on a good whack, but even average players at first division clubs are now on ridiculous wages. It's gone way out of control and there's no way anyone can justify getting paid so much for just kicking a ball about."

This is the kind of grumble usually issued from among the overcoats in the stands but they are the words of Stuart McCall, Bradford City's experienced midfield player.

Manchester United is the world's richest football club and — along with its sponsors — rewards its playing staff accordingly.

Three current players, David Beckham, Roy Keane and Ryan Giggs, are multi-millionaires, while every member of the first-team pool is at least a millionaire or a millionaire-to-be. They are not unique. More than 500 footballers are signed to the 20 clubs in the Premier League. They earn an average of £8,000 per week. Even the lowest paid would need just five seasons to reach millionaire status if they avoided injury and invested wisely. They are all millionaires, united.

Only pop music can match football in its potential to create gilded youth. Of the present 100 richest under-30s in the United Kingdom, 15 are drawn from pop and seven from football. Notably, eight of these pop stars are from Take That or the Spice Girls — groups established in the mid-1990s before the music industry was hit by recession. The business of football, meanwhile, has thrived and salaries are rising by 35 per cent each season in the Premier League.

An agent is at the axis of a footballer's life with a brief to maximise earning potential while ensuring his life is free of the ennui that clutters most of our lives. They also provide a one-stop service for the other ancillary personnel. In pop music this kind of communality has existed since the mid-1960s. The Rolling Stones, for example, had, among others, Tony Sanchez to procure the drugs, Prince Rupert Loewenstein to oversee the finances and Les Perrin to manage the press. The system clearly worked. The group has a combined wealth of £400 million.

These wheeler-dealers and Mr Fix-Its prefer the shadows. They know that the greatest wealth is accumulated stealthily. It is no coincidence that the UK's most successful agent is its most discreet. Tony Stephens is managing director of SFX Sports Group (Europe) Ltd, based in the West Midlands, a company representing a host of star players including Alan Shearer, David Beckham, Michael Owen and Dwight Yorke.

Stephens was a keen amateur footballer — 'a dainty sort of player' in the words of a contemporary — who turned out most Sundays in the late 1970s for Martini International, a team run from a pub in West Bromwich. He was so taken by the life that he wrote a book, *The Sunday Footballer*, with a foreword by Cyrille Regis, the former West Bromwich Albion striker.

Rob Bishop of the *Birmingham Post* and Dave Harrison of the *News of the World* are the only journalists with any real dialogue with Stephens, and this is often circumspect.

"He tends to be very private," said Bishop. "He likes to do these multi-million pound deals away from the glare of the public. I first met him nearly 20 years ago and you had the sense back then that he would move on to higher things. He had something about him."

Stephens is typical of a new generation of agents that replaced the dilettantes who formerly 'represented' footballers — well-meaning friends, solicitors and accountants among them. These could arrange an attendance at a local fete and reply to supporters' letters but dealing with commercial monoliths was another matter. Among this silver-tongued breed Stephens is far from dainty. He negotiated Beckham's seven-year, £4 million deal with Adidas and tied up Shearer with Jaguar, McDonald's and Lucozade.

"He's looked after my lad really well," said Ted Beckham. "I can only comment on how he has been with us and that has been superb. I'm not going to take a pop at other agents."

Most agents have served an apprenticeship of sorts. Stephens became commercial manager of Aston Villa in 1983, at the age of 35. He left in 1986 to become marketing director of Wembley Stadium, promoting leading sports events and concerts by the likes of Michael Jackson and Madonna. He founded Tony Stephens Associates (TSA) in 1988 with David Platt, then a Villa player, as his first client. His efficacy in transfer negotiations involving Platt's moves to three Italian clubs and Arsenal was noted and his roster of star names grew until, in September 1998, TSA was sold for more than £2 million to the American marketing company, Marquee. Just weeks later Marquee merged with the US entertainment group, SFX, creating a company valued at $1 billion.

Such high-octane, high-finance trading is evidence of football's globalisation and its alliance with mainstream entertainment. In the past few years the US blueprint of sports marketing has been increasingly applied to the UK. In the States they view the maxim that a sportsman is secondary to the club for which he plays as archaic. They focus on the individual, package him, then sell the self-created legend as product. Occasionally they have a stake in clubs but this is not always necessary when they exert influence by owning the vital peripheries: the competitions in which they play and the television and merchandising rights.

Two years ago Beckham joined forces with Alan Edwards, long-term media representative of David Bowie and, more germane, publicist for the Spice Girls. Edwards's company, the Outside Organisation, is a showbiz PR heavyweight with nightclubs and fashion designers augmenting a client list that also includes Sir Elton John, Boyzone and a handful of sports interests. Privately, Stephens is unlikely to have welcomed this external influence, but both he and Edwards present a united front.

"In America, whether it be baseball or football, it is not uncommon to have a team of people around a sports star," said Edwards. "It's pretty standard and a perfectly natural development."

Interestingly, Edwards's fee to represent Beckham is paid by adidas, revealing the zeal with which sponsors wish to manage a player's public profile.

The investment in football by adidas, Coca-Cola and McDonald's has coincided with BSkyB's extensive coverage and drawn US entertainment giants to the money pot. Previously they considered it small-time and insular. Their tactic is manifest: collect the players, own the sport.

The Outside Organisation receives 'no fewer than 10' calls per day about Beckham though this escalated to 'almost 150' when he had his recent change of hairstyle. Thongs and sarongs form the bulk of calls.

"Some of them are beyond belief but we try to be polite and positive," said Edwards.

He concedes that Beckham's public profile is 'very much thought about'. He has done just four press interviews in the past two years and the choice of publications reveals much in the branding that Outside wants to achieve — GQ, *The Sunday Times*, *Time Out* and *The Times*. Rather quaintly, Sir Alex Ferguson, the Manchester United manager, once offered Beckham use of a small office at the club from where he could conduct his off-field affairs, perhaps with the help of an assistant.

The traditional football industry has scant regard for agents. Much of this antipathy is because they are viewed as outsiders breaching a cosy boot-room kingdom. Clubs, however, have exploited players since the professional code was established. Many old pros complain that they were treated little better than livestock — underpaid, shunned when injured, moved on when past their best.

Some current players, including Beckham's team-mate at United, Gary Neville, feel that the improvement in the players' lot is due to the rise in football's profile rather than the effectiveness of agents.

"I don't really believe in agents. They come along just as you make it and take 10 to 15 per cent of what you earn. I think it's a disgrace to be honest," he said.

Neville negotiated his own contract and his 'team' included himself, his father — Neville Neville, club secretary at Bury FC — and his accountant. He used the accountancy giant, Grant Thornton. Paul Brookes, based in its Manchester office, looks after a handful of United players and the company acts as auditor for the club. The Professional Footballers' Association is another source of advice with a team of six financial experts.

"As a rule footballers are fairly cautious," said Des Bremner, its financial executive. "They don't like to invest in volatile areas. We talk to them about high interest bank accounts and things like that but some are also involved in commercial and off-shore property investment."

Another method of salting money away is through the formation of companies. Alan Shearer, Britain's wealthiest footballer with a personal fortune of £15 million, is a co-director of Shearer Promotions Ltd with his wife, Lainya. Shearer lives in a converted mill house valued at £1 million in Ponteland, a few miles north of Newcastle, replete with a stream running through its grounds. Both he and his wife have top-of-the-range Jaguar cars.

Limited companies are duty bound to lodge their financial records in the public domain but this information is often partial and selective. The figures available for Shearer Promotions Ltd date back to October 1998 and fail to list turnover and net profit, though they do reveal a 'latest net worth' of £83,000. It appears that most of Shearer's money is invested with the Northern Rock building society and locals joke that he 'helps to keep them afloat'.

It is the ostentatious spending of the Manchester United players, however, that has drawn most attention. Ryan Giggs paid thousands to have the tiles in his swimming pool engraved with the three-feathers emblem of Wales; Dwight Yorke hired a chauffeur to drive his Aston Martin while was he was disqualified; some reportedly need walkie-talkies to find their partners in their palatial homes, such as Beckham's £2 million Rowenbury Mansion in Hertfordshire.

"They are trying to show their peer group that they are successful and they do this in inappropriate ways," said Dr Cary Cooper, a professor of psychology and health. "They buy houses with six bedrooms when they are not even married and could still be living at home with their parents."

Shearer, famously, left Gosforth High School with one CSE in Oral English, which is a marked contrast to most sportsmen in the United States who graduate via the college sports network and seldom turn professional before the age of 21.

"It's ludicrous to call these British kids who play football 'professionals'," said Cooper. "Sure, they might be once they get on the pitch but otherwise they are working-class kids, away from their families and support network, with lots of disposable income and time on their hands. In the circumstances most do remarkably well considering these factors."

Chris Neill is at the frontline for gauging the combustibility of wealth, fame and youth. He is a freelance photographer who has spent the last 11 years working in Manchester supplying 'grab' shots — non-posed photographs to newspapers. Initially footballers were hardly in demand but photographs of United players, especially out of their playing kit, are now highly prized.

"It's different with every player. Some don't give me very good treatment while others are great. Teddy Sheringham is a wonderful professional and Dwight Yorke is a lovely bloke.

Ryan Giggs is always good with me, as well. He has a lovely smile and nearly always makes a great picture," Neill said.

He can earn £500 for a good showing in a tabloid.

"It's difficult though," he said. "United want to be involved in everything. The players get paid a fortune for set-up jobs with magazines where they fly them off to Barbados or somewhere and give them £10,000 for the privilege."

Ferguson, once a rugged centre forward with various Scottish clubs, played at a time when a footballer's outside interests stretched to, say, a part-ownership of a window cleaning round or the obligatory pub. According to Gary Neville, he now tells his young charges:

"Get on with your football, work hard at it and don't worry about the money, because it will follow on naturally."

And it does.

---

* This piece is particularly dated. Much of what it contained, however, was new information in 2000. *The Times* gave over a full broadsheet page which was highly unusual and it was also re-run verbatim in *Four Four Two*.

These days it is common knowledge that football is in league with big business and that players consider themselves to be mini-PLCs. No one seems to question the partnership.

WHEN LOVE BREAKS DOWN

The Times, Saturday 12 January, 2002

Times' writers are asked to nominate their
greatest sporting loss ...

Monday morning, some time in 1974. It's here! On the mat
behind the front door! The football comic with all the excla-
mation marks! Great!

Scorcher was close on perfection. Boy, were you there, shinpad
to shinpad with Bobby Booth (Bobby of the Blues), Nipper
Lawrence (Nipper) and Jack and Jimmy Chelsey (Jack and
Jimmy—what else?).

These were real football folk, slugging it out against teams
with names you never doubted, such as Ironcastle, Merseaport
and Marshness. No gimmicks here, pal. Just raw-boned, inky
action drawn and devised by people clearly in awe of the beautifully bruising game.

Inevitably the Grand Beast heralding the evils of conglomer-
ation, rationalisation and 'you're-all-for-the-sack, lads' came
a-knocking. Childhood offered no safe haven. The Grand Beast
in this case was *Tiger*, a rival comic that cheerfully annexed our
beloved *Scorcher*. Oh Lord, the pain. Suddenly we had to endure
other sports when all we really wanted was football and to hell
with Red Indian wrestlers and their 'beatnik pals' or posh blokes
rallying through the desert in a marvellous Mini.

It got worse. Billy Dane (Billy's Boots), a refugee from *Scorcher*, was re-drawn and started to look wan and worryingly vacant. Luckily they didn't have drugs tests back then. They even had a comic strip about a girl (yuk!) called Tallon of the Track who raced for the Flying Ospreys speedway team. Like, sure!

I cancelled my order. I could think of better ways to spend my five new pence. So there!

ALL QUIET ON THE
PRESTON FRONT

The Times, Monday 14 October, 2002

Darn it, Dollywood. The theme park endorsed by the first lady of country, Dolly Parton, had 2.5 million visitors last year. Much further east, ding-ding, move-along-the-bus, the London Transport Museum will see its entrance turnstile spin 200,000 times in 2002.

Now, no disrespect to collectors of generously proportioned dolls fringed in gingham or lovers of vintage omnibus number plates, but this news should alarm football fans. While they, and most museum-cum-attractions in between, are prospering our National Football Museum appears to be struggling.

The Preston-based (yes, Preston) museum has had just 40,000 visitors in its first year and many believe that a move to London or Manchester might make better commercial sense. Some are muttering that it could even go the way of Sheffield's ill-fated National Centre for Popular Music and close altogether. It might be an oversight but the last news item on its official website is five months old and clicking on 'forthcoming events' draws a blank.

The claim is that national museums and the provinces do not make for wedded bliss. While Deepdale, the home of Preston North End, may seem an odd location, it has a sound historical basis. Preston were the first winners of the Football League in 1888–89 so it is authentic dubbin and liniment country. True enough, but the real basis for its location is probably because the museum's founding team happens to live nearby. And why can't they — and their kind — have something like this close to home? Tough luck, you fancy folk in London.

Unfortunately the playing field isn't level. They're kicking uphill against the wind. Unlike the other 19 British national museums, admission is not free. This is a bureaucratic anomaly it hopes to address but until then adults pay £6.95 and children, £4.95.

Soon after opening last June, numbers were hit by the outbreak of foot-and-mouth disease and Railtrack's policy of reducing train speeds which extended journey times. People who were expected to stop off on their way to the Lake District didn't because the Lakes were effectively out of bounds.

While all this has clearly hit attendance figures, the fact remains that there has been virtually no walk-up support, unlike if it had been based in the centre of a big city. During my three-hour visit last week only two or three people shadowed me around the exhibits and I had the distinct impression that I was the first person to wander into the cafe and shop. Maybe some fans mistakenly believe it is a museum dedicated solely to Preston North End. Or it could be that fans are insular, concerned only with their team's history and next match.

"We could have made it easier for ourselves," sighs Mark Bushell, the museum's marketing manager, acknowledging its geographical disadvantage. Not that Bushell and his team is downbeat, for they are searching for sponsors and plan a new marketing drive. They also strenuously deny the closure rumours.

They deserve to succeed because it is a fantastic place. The curators have reconciled the contrary nature of the game, melding the gritty with the artistic, the grim (the Hillsborough disaster) with the giddy (inflatable bananas). The artefacts are top-notch, among them a shirt worn in England's first international match in 1872; Bert Trautmann's neck-brace from the 1956 FA Cup Final; and the crossbar struck by Geoff Hurst in the 1966 World Cup final. Clearly, it is a collection assembled by football folk, people who know instinctively that the game is sentimental, idiosyncratic, silly and life affirming.

Its real strength and one that might be lost should it move elsewhere is its innate atmosphere. It is a large, dimly lit cave; a majestic secret world where, when you've long gone home, you can imagine Billy Meredith leaping from his photo for a kick-about with Sir Stanley Matthews while Kenneth Wolstenholme commentates. Hopefully he won't get to that bit about some people being on the pitch, they think it's all over.

BOTTLE-FED GENERATION

The Times, Monday 18 October, 2004

It's a goal! A one yard tap-in, miss-hit at that, but stand well back — here comes the celebration. The kid charges down the pitch, head thrown back, arms outstretched. I hope he's not going to do what I think he is. Oh God, he has. He's slid on his knees across a very hard and dry sports hall floor. The sobs echo around the room as someone sends for a brush to clean up the anatomical debris.

I'm here because my two lads, aged five and seven, are all grown-up now. They're through with three-and-your-ins with me in the back garden. They want the real thing: full kit, proper coaching, big matches, water bottles, more water bottles. So, it's another of life's milestones. For them and for me too. I've made it at last; I'm SoccerDad.

Millions of us are at it. Mums too. All of us spending Saturdays or Sundays (or both) on the touchline, thinking it was only five minutes ago when we were out there ourselves. The kids have only just kicked off but, at best, it's half-time for us in life's Match of the Day.

We arrive at the sports centre early on a Saturday morning, 8.30 early. Manchester United and Arsenal shirts begin to file past. I count four Rooneys, three Van Nistelrooys, two Henrys and no Djemba-Djembas. Two kids are wearing Brazil shirts with 'Carlos' printed across their skinny shoulders. I despair,

209

shake my head. Where's the originality of thought? Who's root-ing for the underdog? Then I realise that my eldest is — replete in the kit of our local Coca-Cola League Two club. A group has gathered around him. They might be laughing. That'll build his character. Or destroy it. I managed okay didn't I — *didn't I*?

I notice that all the kits are up-to-date and brand new. No Billy Caspers here, snivelling into their cuffs, hanging on to shorts the size of bed sheets. I'm almost nostalgic for a bit of poverty, some of that make-do spirit. Where have all the poor people gone? Maybe a kid's soccer kit is now viewed as one of life's essentials, the same as a mobile phone, DVD player, satel-lite television and four cans of Special Brew. There's probably a form you can get from the Post Office to make a claim.

The coach has them dribbling slowly to the centre of the hall and back again. After five minutes of this, the kids race en masse to a raft of plastic water bottles at the side. They do this again after a few minutes of playing three-yard passes to one another. These kids are thirsty. Must be hard work all that passing. Now, when I were a lad you'd go through six weeks of school holidays bombing around on your Chopper in scorching heat and sur-vive adequately on a few sips of blue pop. Whole world's gone soft.

Teams are picked and Jack, a lad in my youngest's class at school, is thrown a blue bib. It's a man-sized one and comes down to his knees. Being five is a funny age. Some, like my son, are already quite savvy (he thinks he's black and American and from the 'hood, God help us) while others, like Jack, are still dreaming of Lego castles and hold Spud from *Bob the Builder* as a kind of deity. As the game progresses wildly around him, Jack wanders aimlessly, the lost boy at Waterloo Station. He is so placid amid the chaos, it almost forms a religious tableaux and this notion is enhanced considerably by the bib-cum-cassock he is wearing and the way he fiddles with his hands beneath it. He's probably got some rosary beads under there.

After the first match they sit down, take a rest and gulp madly on their logo-emblazoned bottles. It is clearly one of the absolute rules of childhood that if you gather more than six kids together in one place at least one of them will have a nosebleed. Ryan starts. He's kneeling down in front of my son. No fear, my lad will sort him out, get some help. We've brought him up well. The blood continues to flow. My son stares. And carries on staring. Ryan's shirt has gone from England home to England away. My kid remains unmoved. Finally, one of the others gets up and walks languidly over to Coach:

"Sir, Ryan is bleeding."

Being new to the gang of dads and mums strung along the side, I'm not sure of the proper etiquette. I suppose I should make an effort. I recognise one of the dads from school and notice that his son is left-footed. I say the thought aloud:

"Left-footed, eh?"

"He's two-footed, actually."

It's soon clear which kids have had extracurricular coaching from their dads. When the ball strays into their path they begin a complex series of manoeuvres around it that seem based on a mathematical formula, such is the slide rule precision. This finesse holds no truck with the madding crowd charging after the ball. Howling like banshees, they crash the ball away, anywhere, anyhow. The kid looks at his dad, bewildered:

"You never warned me about that lot."

I'm desperate not to be Competitive Dad but something is bothering me out there. My eldest has been told to play in defence. But he has dropped so deep that he's actually behind the goalkeeper, almost tangled up in the netting. I don't know whether to offer him some advice or laugh it off. Eventually I wave him forward. Hell, he thinks I'm beckoning him over. As one of his opponents races towards goal, he ignores him completely and saunters over to me.

"What, dad?"

"You're playing too deep."

Obviously, he doesn't understand what I'm saying. As he waits for me to explain further, the lad behind him slots the ball home and the cheese-grating of the knees begins all over again.

"Dad," he moans. "I could have stopped him then if you hadn't shouted me over."

A few minutes later the whistle blows and the session for the under-eights finishes. My lads come over, red-faced and out of puff.

"Did you enjoy that?" I ask.

"Yeah, but we're really thirsty."

THE BOY-WAIF AND
THE COLOSSUS

The Times, Monday 11 September 2006

Book review:
Best and Edwards, Football, Fame and Oblivion
by Gordon Burn (Faber)

The day after the death of Sir Matt Busby in 1994, camera crews roamed the concrete prairies surrounding Old Trafford. They found their Everyman and his Everyson. They were both wearing puffa jackets.

"How do you feel about Sir Matt dying?"

"Devastated."

"What did he mean to you?"

"He was like a grandfather to my lad," says the bloke, pointing to his blank-faced kid.

"Did you know him, then?"

"Not personally, no."

This is sport's dilemma incarnate: the perpetual seesaw between queasy sentimentality and a joyous but rational siphon of emotion. Gordon Burn has bravely taken on two of football's most iconic and tragic figures in George Best and Duncan Edwards, two players over whom supposedly strong men have wept oceans.

Edwards was the boy-colossus from Dudley who played for Manchester United at 16, England at 18 and died at 21 in the

Munich air disaster. George Best was the boy-waif from Belfast who could bamboozle defenders, barmen and blondes. He died twice: the sportsman's death on leaving Manchester United at the age of 27 and the mortal's last year, aged 59.

Scores of books have already been published about them both and Burn's is a spirited résumé of them all with idiosyncratic tics of his own thrown in. He has used Edwards and Best as a frame for a far more enigmatic story than the routine 'compare and contrast'. He draws in ancillary characters such as Busby and Bobby Charlton, indeed the whole village of Manchester United.

Whenever the mood suits (and to hell with narrative) he launches into impromptu essays on celebrity and alcoholism, drizzling names and places randomly over the text: Chelsea to Belfast, Waylon Jennings to The Smiths, Salford to Los Angeles, JG Ballard to Jack London. At times it feels as if he has dashed from a road accident, still dazed and stricken with a kind of intellectual whiplash: all this information, got to get it out. The effect is absorbing if occasionally disconcerting.

The research is thorough. He returns first-hand to Dudley and Manchester, trying to make sense of this broth of nostalgia and sentimentality, plotting what it says about us: our relationship with sportsmen and the past. By far the best section is his account of Best's days slumming it in Salford's Brown Bull pub where, at the height of his fame, he slept in a storeroom among beer crates and ashtrays.

Following on from David Peace's *The Damned Utd*, also published by Faber, Burn's is another compelling book about football. It far transcends the routine one-size-fits-all approach to genre-led sports writing and is instead a splurge of ideas set free. Presumably it will not have been a straightforward synopsis when first pitched to publishers.

"What's it all about, Gordon?"

"This and that, partly sociological, bit of cod psychology, a few literary references, biographical, novelistic. Prosey in places, that kind of thing."

"Sounds a bit muddled."

So it is, much like life itself.

TABLE-TOPPING STAR OF
THE BIG FLICK-OFF

The Times, Monday 16 October, 2006

The Hewitt Cup, it had to be. Stephen Hewitt had all the gear, see: floodlights, stands, scoreboard, St John's Ambulance men — all laid out beautifully on a huge piece of chipboard.

Kids turned up most evenings and filed upstairs to his bedroom. Some could hardly reach the table. One or two used their thumbs, heaven help them. Others only brought nine men, with heads missing or double ankle fractures: out came the Bostik.

I made it to the final against, aptly enough, Hewitt. I won 3–0 but his was the moral victory. I cheated. While he flicked to kick I succumbed to the index finger slide, Subbuteo's greatest felony. He's still grumbling about it now, 25 years later.

We weren't the only ones recreating Wembley or Spotland in back-bedrooms. A survey carried out in 2002 showed that 90 per cent of fathers over the age of 30 have at one time owned a Subbuteo set. The game is as much part of our heritage as Marmite, the Sunday Roast and England losing vital qualifying matches.

While the Hewitt Cup was in progress, none of us stopped to think where the man who invented the game might be on that very night. Well, Peter Adolph could have been at one of several places, most of them pretty exotic. He might have been behind the wheel of his Pontiac Firebird or sailing first-class to New York on the QE2. Or he might have been carousing with his Flamenco-dancer lover or sipping his favourite tipple in a Soho nighterie — a gin and mixed topped with a maraschino cherry. Alternatively he might have been bedded down alone in a spare room in his factory, banished there by his exasperated wife.

Peter Adolph planned to write an autobiography but died in 1994 before he could get anything down. When his son, Mark, came across a folder marked 'Memoirs' in his father's effects he decided to tell it for him in *Growing Up with Subbuteo*. It's some story, framing the rich and restless life of an enigmatic man, part-international playboy and part homespun local business-man.

His first foray into public life was at 21 as a crooner with Oscar Rabin and his Romany Band. The band appeared regularly at the Hammersmith Palais where Adolph ran through standards like *If You Were the Only Girl*. During the war he was a driver at RAF Brize Norton although with typical panache he claimed later he had been a navigator in bombers flying over Berlin.

His first business venture grew out of a deep love of ornithology. He traded in birds' eggs, then a perfectly legal occupation. One evening he was running through his fingers a button that had come off his mother's coat. It had a flat bot-tom and rounded sides and when he fastened a washer to it he realised it was better balanced. He developed the button to in-corporate the figure of a footballer and improve significantly on a game already established called Newfooty.

He placed an advert in *Boy's Own* magazine purely to gauge the level of interest in a new game of table football. He was in New York preparing to value an egg collection when he received a cable from his mother. Postal orders to the value of £7,500 (the equivalent of £200,000 today) had been sent to their home from all points in the UK. He caught the next boat back and, along with his mother and a friend, they set about actually making the game. They bulk-ordered buttons from their local Woolworth's and spent six months fixing and sticking to fulfil orders.

Initially he wanted to call it Hobby but the patents office ruled that this was too vague. He settled instead on Subbuteo, taken from the Latin name for the hobby hawk, falco subbuteo. The demand was sustained and Adolph established a factory in his hometown of Tunbridge Wells, and a team of out-reach workers who were paid £1 and 10 shillings for every 1,000 figures they painted. His first expensive purchase was a sports car, the first of many — a Bristol 400.

As the company expanded he set upon his extravagant lifestyle, sailing regularly on the QE2, spending winter months in Cannes, while still maintaining a watchful eye on his company where he made it his business to know every member of staff. England's World Cup victory in 1966 saw the business rocket and three years later he decided to sell the company to Waddington, for a sum of £250,000, a colossal amount in those days.

"Dad was looking out one day over the factory yard," Mark Adolph says. "And saw someone he didn't know who was working for him. I think he realised it wasn't the same anymore."

Adolph became separated from his wife Pam after a long-term affair with his secretary was discovered. He also had romances with a Flamenco dancer whom he had met in Barcelona and a woman from Tunbridge Wells who was nearly 40 years younger than him.

"He couldn't help himself as far as women were concerned," Mark says. "He could really turn on the charm. It obviously wasn't pleasant for me seeing it and knowing how it upset mum, but he had it down to a fine art. I suppose he was a bit of a bugger really."

Adolph briefly worked on the prototype of a game of table baseball but saw out his last days living at homes he owned in Gibraltar and Spain, where he divided his time between photography and botany, seeking our rare orchids. He returned to England when his wife died, visiting the funeral parlour where he sang *If I Loved You* from the musical *Carousel*, while waving a crucifix over her coffin — they had been to see the show on their first date.

He died himself in 1994 after breaking his hip in a fall at a drinks party at his home in Gibraltar.

Flick to kick

The original cost of a Subbuteo set was the equivalent of 37p and came with chalk to mark out the pitch on an army blanket.

- Hasbro bought the Subbuteo brand from Waddington in 1995.
- The trademark of Subbuteo, usually the distinctive image of a player, has been licensed to Next, mobile phone companies and pub quiz machines.
- Next year Subbuteo will celebrate its 70th anniversary.
- Andrea Piccaluga, a world champion Subbuteo player in the 1980s, had his finger-flicking finger insured for £150,000.
- Hasbro planned to end production in January 2000 but a public outcry prompted a re-think and it was re-launched soon afterwards with 10 teams available, sold exclusively through Toys-R-Us.
- Subbuteo has been mentioned in at least two pop songs — *My Perfect Cousin* by The Undertones and *All I Want For Christmas Is A Dupla Plague Away Kit* by Half Man Half Biscuit.

Mr Subbuteo

- The Adolph family originated in Austria, moving to England more than 150 years ago.
- Peter Adolph had trials for Brentford but was a fan of Queens Park Rangers.
- Among his many cars were a Ford Thunderbird, Chevrolet Chevelle Convertible and a Pontiac Firebird. He ordered a Rolls Royce Silver Shadow in midnight blue but later changed his mind.
- He met Beatles Paul McCartney and Ringo Starr with their manager Brian Epstein and signed a deal to manufacture figurines of the group.
- Leaflets were printed proclaiming Stanley Matthews endorsement of Subbuteo, despite him knowing nothing about it. He threatened legal action and the leaflets were destroyed.
- He was a skilful Subbuteo player himself and often scored direct from corners.

BOB MOUNTFORD

Rochdale programme

Bob Mountford, Rochdale's centre-forward in the late 1970s, died in August, 2008 and I contributed a short piece to the match programme. It forms a fitting end to the book.

It's 1975. It's raining. I'm 10 years old and watching a mediocre Fourth Division football team in a falling-down ground. Older lads are trying to pick fights with rival fans all around me. We lose. I'm fed up. Not going there again, I tell myself. A fortnight later, I break my own promise.

Why? Why did I keep on coming back? Why am I still coming back? It would be an over-statement to say it is down to one man, but not a complete untruth. Bob Mountford was one of very few Rochdale players who, back then, actually seemed to belong on a football pitch. Sure, the others ran about and pushed and shoved, but Mountford had composure, assurance and, most of all, passion. In his three seasons with Dale I never saw him pull out of a tackle or flinch as he careered towards a goalkeeper's outstretched fist. When you saw that Mountford cared, it made you care too. With him in the team, there was always hope and hope is why we keep on coming back, why we're still here.

As a kid, I had a regular correspondence with Mountford. He always replied to my letters; not glib two-word answers but proper, detailed responses. I have written about this in my book *Believe in the Sign*. It meant so much that my hero did this and it played a large part in my wanting to be a writer. Where, in the 1970s, I was assembling the glued-down and typewritten 'Bob Mountford File', by the 1990s, I was working for *The Times*. Bob Mountford was so much part of this journey.

Earlier this year, I finally tracked Bob down and sent a copy of the book to him in Australia where he had been living since the early 1980s. Thirty years on, we began corresponding again, this time via e-mail. Once more, his e-mails revealed a kind, enthusiastic man. His last one, sent in May, saw him enthusing about a couple of young players he felt worthy of a trial at Spotland.

Jane, his wife, e-mailed a few weeks ago to let me know Bob wasn't well and revealed that he had suffered from cancer for the past 12 years. A couple of Sundays ago I received another e-mail from her containing the words 'Beautiful Bobby' in the subject line. I knew, without reading it, what the e-mail was going to tell me.

It might seem strange that Jane should use such a phrase about a footballer who was so aggressive and committed. But to see Bob play, the way he would rise tall and sure at the far post to head the ball goalwards or how he would send the ball dipping and spinning from his in-step into the back of the net was to see beauty suddenly visiting the mundane. Beautiful Bobby, indeed.

BELIEVE IN THE SIGN

Mark Hodkinson

ISBN 1-904590-17-9

Believe in the Sign is about a damp corner of England where nothing much but everything happens. It is a 'sort of' memoir of a normal, average boy who would have grown up happily average and normal but for a dark and perverse passion: the seductive lure of masochistic devotion to a no-hope, near-derelict football club.

But it isn't all joyously uplifting. Swimming through the murk is a swarm of snapshots that bring growing up in the 1970s and 1980s into startling focus. Mad kids and sad kids and good kids from broken homes; teenage wrecking parties; pub brawls; long existential marches along the motorway banking; the baiting of Elton John and a club chairman caught playing 'away from home.'

Then Death bumps into Life. A girl is abducted and the town becomes a cave, the light sucked out. Meanwhile in the sunny shine outside, the future is afoot: cotton mills close down and supermarkets invade; school-leavers evolve into YOP-fodder and everyone's mum is holding Tupperware parties to get the down-payment on a colour telly.

Variously serious and funny, steely-eyed and tender, Hodkinson plumbs the depths but isn't afraid of the shallows. Dip a toe.

THE LAST MAD SURGE OF YOUTH

Mark Hodkinson

ISBN 978-1-904590-20-0

"A good group isn't about everyone being able to play well. You need people to shape it, give it heart. The best bands, the ones that matter, are a group of people singing about their lives, their mams and dads, the streets they came from, the crap jobs they've had, everything. And serving it all up pure to the public, saying, 'This is what we are – do you recognise any of it?' All the better if you were dragged up because punters see a kind of glamour in squalor. Ideally they'd like you to have been brought up by wolves, living half wild on the streets. That's what rock'n'roll is, why bands from these shitty estates get to be massive. And do you know why people like all this? It's because they're envious but rooting for you at the same time. Their own gang – the kids they grew up with – didn't stick together. They see you as someone who made it through and they want to be part of it. That's why they buy the records. It reminds them of what could have been."

The Last Mad Surge of Youth is an intelligent, literate work that sidesteps the usual clichés of rock novels. Its authenticity and authority is never compromised, a viewpoint held dear by punk and new wave. It is also about growing up, friendship, fame, addiction, love. And hope.

POMONA BOOKS

Pomona is a wholly independent publisher dedicated to bringing before the public the work of prodigiously talented writers. Our books can be purchased on-line at:

www.pomonauk.com

Pomona backlist

P-001	1-904590-00-4	*Footnote** Boff Whalley
P-002	1-904590-01-2	*Rule of Night* Trevor Hoyle
P-003	1-904590-02-0	*The Fan* Hunter Davies
P-004	1-904590-03-9	*Love Songs* Crass
P-005	1-904590-05-5	*Sum Total* Ray Gosling
P-006	1-904590-06-3	*Diary of a Hyperdreamer* Bill Nelson
P-007	1-904590-08-x	*The Price of Coal* Barry Hines
P-008	1-904590-09-8	*Looks & Smiles* Barry Hines
P-009	1-904590-12-8	*Kicked Into Touch (plus extra-time)* Fred Eyre
P-010	1-904590-13-6	*Mean with Money* Hunter Davies
P-011	1-904590-10-1	*Zone of the Interior* Clancy Sigal
P-012	1-904590-04-7	*The Arms of the Infinite* Christopher Barker
P-013	1-904590-14-4	*The Second Half* Hunter Davies
P-014	1-904590-17-9	*Believe in the Sign* Mark Hodkinson
P-015	978-1-904590-18-7	*The Not Dead* Simon Armitage
P-016	978-1-904590-22-4	*This Artistic Life* Barry Hines
P-017	978-1-904590-20-0	*The Last Mad Surge of Youth* Mark Hodkinson
P-018	978-1-904590-21-7	*The Richard Matthewman Stories* Ian McMillan & Martyn Wiley
P-019	978-1-904590-25-5	*Down the Figure 7* Trevor Hoyle
P-020	978-1-904590-23-1	*J.D. Salinger: A Life Raised High* Kenneth Slawenski
P-022	978-1-904590-26-2	*My Improper Mother and Me* Esther Fairfax
P-024	978-1-904590-27-9	*Weirdo. Mosher. Freak.* Catherine Smyth

Forthcoming:

P-023	978-1-904590-24-8	*The Celestial Cafe* Stuart Murdoch